Shorelines

Also by Alycia Pirmohamed

Another Way to Split Water

Shorelines

Memory, migration and the selves we become

Alycia Pirmohamed

CANONGATE

First published in Great Britain in 2026
by Canongate Books Ltd, 14 High Street, Edinburgh EH1 1TE

canongate.co.uk

1

British Library Cataloguing-in-Publication Data
A catalogue record for this book is available on
request from the British Library

ISBN 978 1 83726 205 2

Typeset in Garamond by Palimpsest Book Production Ltd,
Falkirk, Stirlingshire

Printed and bound by CPI Group (UK) Ltd, Croydon CR0 4YY

The manufacturer's authorised representative in the EU for product safety is GC Sustainability & Compliance, 7 avenue du Général Leclerc, Paris 75014 (gpsr@baldwinglobalconsulting.com)

In memory of Alnoor Jafferali Pirmohamed
1959–2025

Contents

A Note on Form

STRUCTURALLY, THIS BOOK MOVES LIKE a body moves from land into water. First, there is a section on *Land*, the solid ground beneath your feet: pieces that move more narratively, that are less formally disrupted and more traditional in the way they are read. These are the pieces that look toward the endless prairies, rolling mountains, or thick brush of forests. When you approach the section on *Shoreline*, the place where land and water meet, the book becomes more comfortable with liminal spaces and hybridity. The pieces land neither fully in motifs of land nor water, but somewhere in-between. Thematically, the idea of thresholds and meeting places comes to the fore, cresting in a piece on lighthouses and all they symbolise, the multiple worlds they straddle. In the last section, on *Water*, solid ground gives way to luminous blue, and the pieces float away from any traditional narrative demands. They explore form and are buoyant in their amorphousness. Like a wave breaking onto the shore, these pieces crash with personal disclosures, only to pull them back again into the concealed depths of the ocean. It is here where the body swims.

Prologue

The Woman Who Belongs and Unbelongs in Two Waters

The Indian Ocean

The waters off the coast of Michamvi reflect the russet sunset tones of the sky. I tie back my hair, thick and wiry with salt, and set aside my clothes. The sea beckons me in, and my dark body moves toward its shimmering. I have swum within the watery margins of different places and different memories all my life. Everything in the sea – dense or sleek or sludgy or buoyant or spectral – is a thing beloved. At the water's edge, here at the cusp of a place I want so badly to call my own, I am not tentative. I am not anxious or afraid. It is so easy to glide through the warm water up to my thighs – my waist – my neck.

I look back and Zanzibar across many shades catches my eye. Its rock faces and its verdant foliage stir different desires within me. Naively, I think that whatever trauma has followed me my whole life can't follow me here. The Indian Ocean is an embrace. My name is drawn in the coastal sands by my own hand. My lineage is woven with the reeds, gurgling in the mouths of fish, unstitching slowly like the stalwart mangrove trees that eventually fall as timber into the sea.

The Lake I Can't Remember

What I think I want most is to be recognised – to be welcomed. I desire this conflictual kind of belonging, driven by the desire to assume the shape of someone who is familiar to the white gaze that surrounds me. To assume this shape as a young brown girl who lives in a rural village in northern Alberta is to practise excruciating contortion.

I become everything but myself, and my body hurts from the strain. There are so many eyes that want to affix me into a digestible narrative, and so, I let them. I'm ten years old and my own identity slips away from my small hands.

I don't want to be a stranger all my life, rivering between the archetypes of welcomed immigrant and dangerous foreigner. Nothing at this crossroads is certain, especially not my own sense of self. Again and again, I feel myself tugged in every possible way, sometimes by my own making.

Self-erasure can feel like a balm as long as I don't try to look back. It's only when looking back that the vast blank emptiness of all that was erased becomes a haunting.

But there are also ghosts here. The ones I know and the ones I don't. They thrash in the waves. The sea harbours secrets. I let them graze my skin and a shiver moves up my body. My family and I have our secrets too. Our ghosts unbend in the water, rising up to greet me like smoke. There are dark stories of families upended and families left behind. These are remnant and marginal notes that accompany accounts of indentured labour, Partition, and forced migration. As East Africa ebbs away from myth and into reality, I reckon with the knowledge I have gained on this trip across many waters. It's 2019, and I'm realising that a firm home, a long lineage, and even a vast and beautiful sea will never fix, as in fix into place, a person. I'm realising that to belong somewhere is a burden.

Five years later, Michamvi blurs like a dream. I am re-examining my diasporic identity, my own disparate borders, according to new experience. I clear off a chair next to the hospital bed and sit beside my father. We do not discuss the phantom limb of home. He was there then too, in East Africa five years ago, relearning his childhood home at sixty years old. Meanwhile, I paddled in the ocean that I treated as a salve for my disobedient heart that never feels at ease. My memory of our trip constantly splits anew. Each time I look back, I replenish the glimmer of the sea with my capable imagination. I can tell its contours are becoming uncanny with every retelling.

East Africa can't be, I decide, the heart of us. This place, this homeland, can't be our centre. Instead, I have to redefine distance, Like the lake I can't remember. I cast my mind back and the margins of emptiness quiver. I concentrate hard, my eyebrows coming together in a frown. I see a flash of sunlight and the glitter of sloshing green water. There is silt or something like it fogging up the mirror of water and turning my reflection murky. My mother is on the shore, laughing at my shrieks that ring out into this translucent memory every time a small fish skates by.

This village is in the cold northeast of the province. I remember my body *in* the water. It must be summertime, or else it would have been too cold to swim—

((

))

There are large swathes of my past that I have purposefully scoured, letting blissful silty murkiness overrun the traumas that wedge deep fissures into my life. *It's okay*, I think, to let the scenic arrival, departure, longing, belonging, and the ocean itself in relation to the knowledge that my father will never be able to go back. His body will no longer allow for it. The centre of a life can't be a place you can never return to. That would be [illegible] too exilic and painful. This admission sits uneasily next to the half-formed plans we made only eight months ago to visit Zanzibar once again. They will remain unformed, amorphous, forever.

I know the feeling of estrangement when it takes the shape of migration. As a second-generation immigrant in Canada, I have always felt the weight of an elsewhere life. This knowingness is mine and I grow around it, like fruit grows around a stone in the natural process of things. This weight is abstract and it aches. It twinges – a little elegiac poem of pain.

Now, leaning forward to hear his quiet voice, I attempt to understand a different kind of estrangement. I find myself grappling and failing to comprehend what it means to never return.

lake, my mother's laughter, and one of my first outdoor swims ebb away into what is unretrievable. These moments of levity, of familial closeness, of childhood happiness, are bound with slurs and violence and fear for my father every time he goes to mosque to pray.

I can't truly remember the beauty of cool water slipping over my body and its reflection. I can't truly remember the lake's edge, the threshold I crossed to get there. I can't truly remember the slippery aqueous kind of belonging to landscape. But I also can't remember the pain.

To articulate them both is, in a way, to make them up completely through the renarrativisation of art and literature. The lake is both real and not real. The lake is a figurative homeland.

It's a kindness, isn't it? To let the abstractedness of what's unknown linger casually in my art rather than to excavate my triggers for the curious onlooker. To do so even when that curious onlooker is myself.

Land

51.1784° N, 115.5708° W

Of homeland sky and homeland green

In Banff, the sky was lavender, the colour of dreaming. I followed the hue until I reached the jagged signature of the Canadian Rockies. The mountains were a perfect scrawl at the base of the sky, a perfect line of poetry. It disappeared – the soft sky, the dream – either obscured by the snow-crowned mountains or hidden by a trespass of fog. I sensed it immediately, the weight that lifted. The constant hard press upon my heart that alleviated at the sight of those tall peaks.

*

Eight years ago, I left Canada for Scotland. When I first left Alberta, I didn't think about all the things that I would forget. My past life slipped away too quickly, and what I recall is often riddled with gaps. I pull at the threads of my memory, retracing my life and unravelling images of a young woman who knew the mountains by name. On a clear day, I could see the Rockies from the small balcony of my apartment in Calgary. Just the crests of them, sure, but there they were. So very solid and ever-present and, in that way, so unlike the ghostliness of memory and history and ancestry. The deep boreal greens of that province were the palette of my childhood, and I took it all for granted. The mountain landscape. The beauty of the plains. The close distance of my family, only a short drive away. There was a whole world contained there that I never allowed myself to see.

I loved the mountains. As an adult, I tried to make up for a childhood of staying away – not purposely, but by circumstance. Though we lived close to them, I grew up in a family that stayed fastened in place by Edmonton, the city in which I was born, rarely venturing further than its surrounding prairielands. So, this return to Banff, a solitary trip taken several years after my move to Edinburgh, felt like a gift.

*

Somehow, that morning was my first time in the mountains alone. I disappeared into the forest at the foot of Sleeping Buffalo and walked the dirt trail unhurriedly. Light poured gently through the arms of surrounding trees. I savoured the stillness of my usually unbridled grief. I savoured everything here. It was mid-October and hiking in the Bow Valley in autumn was akin to witnessing magic. Wine-red aspen leaves crunched underfoot, but the evergreens were abundant and beckoning. Every so often the light glimmered off an emblematic golden larch. I knew if I climbed high enough, I would find entire sweeping forests of them.

Sleeping Buffalo is Banff National Park's smallest mountain. The Blackfoot name for it is Iinii Istako, and its Stoney Nakoda name is Eyarhey Tatanga Woweyahgey Wakân, which translates to its English name, Sacred Buffalo Guardian Mountain. I was staying in an arts centre that lived in this mountain's shadow, and so it was a very short walk to where the trail begins. I made for an early start, eager to remain alone. My steps were the only footprints on the frosted grassland. In my backpack, I carried an extra fleece, a smattering of snacks, and a borrowed copy of Cole Swensen's *On Walking On*.

The hike up Sleeping Buffalo is an in-and-out trail of less than five kilometres. I wanted to cherish every step. I was so rarely back in the Rocky Mountains, and I wanted to commit all its details to my memory. The first time I went up Sleeping Buffalo, the only other time, is awash with uncertainty. All I remember are the switchbacks covered in snow and the young faces of the friends I climbed with.

*

Time passes by differently in the mountains, whether trekking through valleys or while in ascension. It stretches far and wide, making space for thoughts to roam endlessly until they too tire out like a pair of legs. But time can also contract, condensing an impossibly grand landscape embedded with its own deep geological scale into mere hours of walking. The sedimentary rock I stepped over was up to 1.5 billion years old. Like time, I too appeared changed when pinned against the sloping verdure of the natural world. In the mountains, I was caught between the person I knew I was and the one I wanted to be.

It is in that theoretical place where I often find myself: one foot secured in this world and one foot reaching for another. That autumn in Banff, my body loosened itself slowly and sleepily in the Rocky Mountains, all while acknowledging its division into further parts. Some of these were nestled deeply in my other homes. In Edinburgh, but also in those other realms, in the real and imagined versions of places that I belong to in that slippery kind of way anyone belongs anywhere: Alberta, Scotland, Oregon, East Africa, India.

*

For better or worse, willingly or unwillingly, the question of home is my life's preoccupation. It creeps into my body and into my art until it becomes them both. I have always been troubled by what becomes an implicit emphasis on borders – I seem to be forever discontent, an assemblage of fragments, no matter what parcel of demarcated land I end up on. A friend once told me, sometimes a place doesn't feel like home until you leave and return. For a time, her words felt like the truth. With every return to Alberta, a dormant love stirred stronger in my chest. The mountains were there, as were my childhood memories and the silvery lineage of women who looked like me. The glistening flatlands and the openness of the prairies slotted into place. This home was a knowingness.

But as I threaded through the evergreens that morning, I couldn't help but think that it all looked like a foreign country. The question, I realise now, has another side to it: what makes a place a home *and who have I become*? I can't answer one without answering the other. As I began the ascent, crossing the threshold into that first solitary hike in the Rockies, I thought about borderzones. I am suspended, always, between leaving and returning. And the borders I cross are also beholden to the passage of time.

To arrive and depart. To visit and revisit. To leave and return. Passing through borders clarifies the foreignness of a place. Or perhaps it's more accurate to say this constant migration makes me realise the perceived foreignness of myself. I had entered the mountain landscape and somehow that felt like leaving my past self behind. Every face I encountered was the face of a stranger. Every face was a face I could not decipher.

*

Even before I moved to Scotland, I knew myself within the shape of a migrant identity. My father and mother are of South Asian descent and were both born in East Africa, although they didn't meet until they migrated to Canada in the 1970s and '80s respectively. When someone asks me about my heritage, this is the easiest answer: I am a second-generation immigrant. I contain all the border crossings my ancestors made before I was born. I also contain all the accompanying heartaches and pleasures of a fraught multiplicity.

With migration and forced displacement came degrees of loss. With leaving and arriving, with crossing a border, came the fitting of oneself into a new national construct and an awareness of perceived difference. My mother's passport has always had her place of birth scripted neatly on the identification page: Dar es Salaam, Tanzania. It had once seemed so far away. I thought of Tanzania as a stark contrast from my world of Edmonton, Alberta. Especially the latter's northern latitude and unrelenting cold. I had a settler Canadian upbringing, and I assimilated as fully as possible to a country built on imperialism. My sense of belonging as a child was measured by the success of my integration within this context.

*

I remember the story this way: my father was a bachelor who had many girlfriends in his young adult life. My mother was younger, six years his junior at eighteen years old. It was Khushali – Imamat Day – which is a religious ceremony within the Ismaili branch of Islam. The event took place as a boisterous celebration in a community hall in downtown Edmonton with fine dress, good food and various kinds of entertainment.

He met my mother toward the end of the evening. Everyone was enrapt in the movements of dandiya raas and the hall was filled with a swirling, invigorating collage of bodies dressed in elaborate saris. It was the 1980s after all. I imagine the reels of fabric were even more embellished than they might be now, glinting with an excess of ornaments and golden embroidery. Amidst all the excitement, all the electric dancing, all the dandiya sticks echoing in unison with their percussive sound, he saw her and he fell in love.

Before that, before my parents met and budded off from their distinctive families to create what would turn out to be a tumultuous life together, they lived separate lives in Edmonton. For years there was a wide, reaching landscape of snow between them.

*

I have spent long swathes of my adult life asking my parents about East Africa. My impulse to ask questions comes from a place both genuine and insincere. For much of my childhood, I tried to forget any details about my inherited migration. In Canada, a nation where Western consciousness and whiteness hold power, I'd experienced enough racism and Islamophobia to value whiteness above all. I desired a life uncomplicated by my Muslim upbringing, my hard-to-place first language, and the confusion and self-doubt that I had internalised as a racialised person.

By the time I wanted to undo the damage caused by the colonial context within which I was raised, I was an adult who had strayed very far from the centre of my familial inheritance. So much, I felt, had been lost to that gaping hole that continued to widen as I looked away. What I didn't know at the time was that, unlike some countries, Tanzania doesn't allow a person to hold dual citizenship. In order to be Canadian, my parents and their descendants have relinquished their legal identities as East Africans. This kind of exile, legislative and officiated by border control, felt final in a way that abstractions like inheritance and memory and poetic refrain never do. Once I learned this, I became interested in my family history with new vigour.

The insincerity is this part. The artmaking born from traversing cultural and national discord. The archival process that, although it is born from wanting to *keep*, accelerates certain losses. It is impossible to keep everything. What remains and for whom? I know a beautiful, enticing product when I see one. I have always loved to create with language. I'm coming to terms with how to unlearn again: how to archive under my own terms rather than for the spotlight of another's gaze.

I am pressing hard into the wound of these questions. How can I interrogate the societal expectation that is tied to the action of 'homing' in a Western country? How do I stop from falling prey to the alluring restraints of assimilation?

*

The place my parents were born, the single, resolute fact that, according to the dictionary, decides my 'homeland', does not fully exist. Just like my memories of the Canadian Rockies and the untranslatable version of my past self, my parents' birthplace is an ever-changing collection of impressions.

I plunder libraries and papers and forum posts and learn that the name I know, Tanzania, only came into existence in 1964, just one year before my mother was born. Formerly, the region was known as Tanganyika, and even this name is a remnant put into use by the earlier German colonisers. My homeland is tinged by the imagination of others. New knowledge constantly revises my understanding. I realise with a surge of unease that the 'other' includes me, in my struggle to breach the silence of my family's dissipating memory.

My curiosity and my searching have widened the chasm between me and those elsewhere places I thought were in some way my own. It is a reminder that an ancestral homeland is not held in stasis or inheritance. Within the slippery bends of my diasporic experience, I can make the mistake of only ever viewing it through the lens of myself and my own enfolded past.

*

There was no snow as I climbed Sleeping Buffalo, though across the way I saw the tops of the taller mountains in the Bow range. They seemed to lift the landscape, inviting my gaze to travel far beyond the forest floor to where their white crowns caught the light. Every step forward was a counter force to the time I spent hunched up at my studio desk or bent over a book – or worse, endlessly scrolling my devices.

Because of its relatively low elevation, hiking up Sleeping Buffalo is popular all year long, even now, in the autumnal months, when the weather was turning. It meant that erosion of the trail was continuous, the paths exposed to almost constant footfall, a treading and re-treading of the mountain's lithic story.

*

My knowledge of my ancestors' migrations and my family's lives in Tanzania is a blur. I'm afraid of excavating further. I can't exactly place where this fear comes from. Perhaps I'm worried that a firm knowledge will break the fragile glass that is my identity. I have built a precarious sense of self around ambiguity, buoyed by my own fascination with renarrativisation, untraceable lineage and gaps in memory.

Perhaps I'm afraid of embarking on this grand search for self and ancestral understanding only to come up empty handed. Or worse, with the feeling that it all doesn't matter as much as I hope it will. Maybe it's better to live with swerving questions and the potentiality of answers rather than delving into the mysterious lake of my history and retrieving nothing satisfactory when I come up for air.

*

The less convenient answer to the question of heritage is that my parents' birthplace is a mingling: of memories, of misrememberings, of lost documents, of familial gravesites, of colonial exploration, and of gaps and blank spaces. All of this, too, was inherited from their own parents and grandparents who also journeyed from one country to another.

Although the brushstrokes of their childhoods are not the same rich depths of boreal green, my parents have lived in Canada now for the vast majority of their lives. I think of them as the steadfast link to my ancestral homeland, as the cultural stronghold that ties me to Tanzania. As so unequivocally from that country I want to know. The truth is, they have lived in Alberta for so long now. Their time near the Canadian mountains has and will always far exceed my own.

*

In my imagination, I can cut out the rare image from one of my own memories of my father in the mountains of Jasper, Alberta, during a dry summer of my childhood. I transpose him to the coastal edges of Tanzania, where I know he once regularly felt his feet sink into the sand. This strange, pieced-together, hybrid, real-unreal image coalescing environments becomes a memory as true as any of my others. Despite being Canadian-born, I can almost imagine my body as permanently there too, tinged with salt spray and slippery verdant foliage that I cannot name.

*

The use of the word 'diaspora' exploded in the 1980s. It became a staple concept in transnational studies and was used as an inconvenient marker of multiplicity and dislocation. Early definitions were inextricable from displacement, loss and exile. These feelings were so tied to the concept that they still resonate today. 'Diaspora' is an alluringly broad, almost phantomic notion to apply to the emotional narratives that accompany immigration. I think this holds true from first-generation immigrants to second-generation immigrants and beyond.

I exist within multiple diasporas, and so I also exist within intersecting socioeconomic, political and cultural conditions across multiple nations. The word 'diaspora' represents a journey that is multidirectional. Until recently, I had never visited what would typically be called my homeland. My diasporic journey constantly shifts. It is reimagined and transformed over time. It collects new meanings and understandings and, as such, previous understandings are re-examined and revisited. A diasporic identity is necessarily an ephemeral one.

*

I gather anecdotes from family members to momentarily satisfy the magnetic pull I feel toward Tanzania. My father often recounts periods of his young life with boyish energy. He tells me small, ostensibly mundane things, like his childhood nicknames and how his neighbourhood friends would praise his football skills, screaming out 'Shockie Shockie!' (always said twice), as he dribbled the ball. There were also small, sensorial memories like the nightly ritual that his mother continued long into his childhood of oiling his hair until he reeked of coconut.

Encounters with my father's past are both inherited memory and inherited experience. I can hear his beautifully melodic voice and his laugh every time I delve back into those moments. The sound emanates in my childhood memories of Edmonton. It catches in the imagined odours of Tanzania, rustles in the Edinburgh wind, and finds me trailside on Sleeping Buffalo. My body flickers in the light between gaps of lodgepole pine. These stories shaped me, even if I can never know exactly how. They sink into my body and become the way I move. They are my legacy.

*

Those processes that we associate with the natural world, like decay, regeneration, mutation and new growth, contribute to the legibility of colonial histories. Colonised lands were viewed by colonialists as empty space: land to experiment on, land to clear, land to cultivate. Writer and literary critic Edward Said argued that to think and write about homeland as a process of recovery and mythmaking is enabled first and foremost by the land. When I evoke the notions of homeland and diaspora, I am evoking the natural world in both a literal and a figurative sense.

In the 1940s, British colonialists cleared bush land in Tanzania in order to cultivate peanuts for seed oil. Local agricultural methods were ignored in favour of machinery that didn't suit the terrain, and plans failed to consider the soil type and rainfall of the region. This groundnut scheme was a disaster and the colonisers abandoned it. Some scars remain on the land while others become buried in the ecosystem's own self-cycling or under new economic endeavours on the landscape.

The earth is a site of extraction and colonial exploitation. It holds and recycles and submerges memories of migration and human violence. Nature is an archive where conquest and war can be read and examined.

*

Since the 1980s, the term 'diaspora' has itself been changing. I think it is being productively reinvented and reimagined according to new ideas and articulations of experience. Formerly, the concept had a strong attachment to the idea of origins and an exile's dispersal from a single nation. This separation was often expressed as a nebulous tangle of nostalgia and a lament to go back, not only geographically but temporally. Diaspora was the yearning to return to a version of the past and the inability to do so.

In an increasingly globalised and especially digitalised world, these concrete and nostalgic representations of diaspora are again becoming transient. They are only applicable some of the time. As much as it is anchored to place, and consequently to nation, the concept of diaspora slides into the post-national. This is happening alongside rising critiques of national identity and borderlands. The diasporic identity is fluid. In these new formations, it lacks borders and in fact may even refute them. Boundaries extend beyond dimensions of space and time. Knowledge lifts off one person's internet search and onto another's sense of self.

*

I was aware that at the top of Sleeping Buffalo was an unobstructed vista in all directions. There was the hope, the kind that perhaps follows any climb, that I would arrive at the top and see *further*, somehow beyond the borders of myself. I wanted the summit to provide the clarity I always longed for, the ability to know and understand all directions. That knowledge, I thought, eluded me as a woman who constantly zigzagged through time and space, memory and erasure shaping spectral landscapes around her.

But before the top, before the arrival, there was the gradual upward slope. Grey, ancient rock hugged either side of the trail, and from in between the brush, I caught glimpses of the Bow River down below. It snaked through the valley, connecting multiple places and moments in time as well as evading them.

At seeing the valley in snapshots, my hope multiplied, fastening itself to not only the climb, but also the river's wandering and captivating journey.

*

Dandiya raas is the folk dance of Gujarat. I didn't know its origins as a child, and now I can't remember when I played dandiya last. All I knew then was a vibration that began in my body and flowed outward, pouring into the bamboo sticks we'd hold and strike against one another. The traditional knowledge of the steps was a bodily kind, and it came with the act of doing – with being swept down the line by the person next to you, sometimes a stranger, and with sensing the rhythm of the music as it compelled you to step back, to lift your arm, to turn. Eventually, we would all become one dazzling, flowing mass, totally in sync.

When I imagine this folk dance of my past, I think of my parents meeting amidst the array of bodies. My mother is always front and centre of the memory. Her red lipstick, the smell of her treasured J'adore perfume, the feel of her curly hair. I see her body rotating just before the satisfying sound of the dandiya sticks finding their partner with a loud *crack*.

My parents were born into plurality. The passing down of this folk dance from Gujarat to, eventually, my own body reminds me that, like second-generation immigrants in the West, they were also navigating their own diasporas as Indians born in East Africa. What I know and have grown up with is a cultural synthesis of Tanzanian and Indian knowledges and practices. The Kachchh landscape of our ancestors was my parents' ancestral homeland.

And yet, while I feel a rhizomatic connection to my ancestral homeland in India, together with a longing to know more and possibly even fit my Westernised body within it, I don't see this desire mirrored in my parents. I wonder at why. Perhaps they perceive their homeland as not a physical nation state, but rather a metaphysical religious community with its own strong multinational identity. Or, relatedly, perhaps it's because Hindu nationalism and religious tension made it difficult for Muslims in East Africa to identify with their past ties to India, particularly given that the region of Gujarat is right at the border, just below Pakistan.

*

I feel unmoored. I lack clarity about my family's inter-generational migration and I'm envious of others who have more tangible artefacts from their ancestors' lives. Once, I looked up my grandfather's name and found just a single record: his gravesite at Rockyview Garden of Peace in Calgary, Alberta.

When storytelling is no longer an option, I pull from existing archives collected by people I have never met. I want to understand my family's migration – its errant pattern over centuries – but have little access to primary sources. I find retellings of other familial accounts, trawl through forum posts, read ethnographic research, history papers, and so on. I recoil from asking extended family members who I barely know about their lives in Tanzania. I'm afraid of excavating and I'm afraid of translating other lives into my writing for consumption. Much of what I have found out over time, I've withheld from this space.

I fill in the considerable gaps of whatever else is missing with imagination. Like Dionne Brand writes in *A Map to the Door of No Return*: 'any wisp of dream is evidence.'

*

Canada's colonial legacy and its ongoing violence is evident in the cartography of the Rocky Mountains. Sleeping Buffalo, or Sacred Buffalo Guardian Mountain, has another name. A colonial moniker overwrote its Indigenous names in the mid-nineteenth century. Though called Sleeping Buffalo for generations, in the 1880s, it was 'officially' renamed Tunnel Mountain.

There is no tunnel in this small mountain. The name stuck after surveyors for the Canadian Pacific Railway considered blasting a tunnel for their railroad project through the Bow Valley. This tunnel never existed, but its colonial imprint remains on the landscape: in the ghostliness of the tunnel that never was and in the tracks that curve a route around the mountains instead, marking areas of settlement that upended the Bow Valley in other ways.

*

Throughout history, diasporic communities have dispersed across the globe in response to colonising powers. In my ancestral homelands – both in South Asia and East Africa – patterns of migration were tied steadfastly to the land and who controlled it. From conversations over time, I've gleaned that my paternal grandfather's family hailed from the northwest region of India that now borders Pakistan. My father once told me the name of the small village where his father was born and where his relatives resided as pastoral inhabitants during British colonial rule: Nagalpur. His lineage is one of labourers who worked on tough and infertile soil. They spoke a language with a borrowed written form, a language that descended far down my family tree and eventually found its way onto my tongue. My own first language, Kutchi.

I have always thought of my life as scattered. Wayward. A series of broken lines or a river without a middle. When I learn that my first language traces all this way back, passing through centuries,

I feel grounded in a way I'm not accustomed to. A new sting occurs. A pain resurfaces that I thought I had moved on from: the ache of no longer being able to speak it.

*

It's difficult to find information about Nagalpur specifically. For a long time, I had been looking up the wrong name, either misspelled or misremembered by my father, or perhaps changed since the stories of the village were passed down to him so long ago. But of the surrounding region, the Kachchh region, I came to know topographical features. I read about the perennial shortage of water and how, back then, there was no presence of a navigable river. This region was a generally barren land, unable to support even stalks of grain, which forced its inhabitants to look out toward sea. To the possibility of leaving.

My bapa, the real figure outside of these narratives and imagined sojourns, died when I was five years old. I see flashes of him when I think hard, but it's very difficult to imagine him as a young boy on the withering farmlands of Nagalpur. Because he is no longer here, because none of my grandparents are, I find myself processing my history through figurative truths and someone else's accounts. I house myself in articles about the migratory influence of the Indian Ocean and monsoon winds.

*

Just before reaching the summit of Sleeping Buffalo, I saw a herd of elk pass by far below. I watched them for as long as I could, before they moved together into the thick fringe of evergreen trees at the foot of a neighbouring mountain. It felt special to see them. It unlocked something in me, like running into a very old friend who had since taken on the shape of a stranger. In the image of the elk, I saw my younger self. This self was so attuned with the montane ecosystem, so entangled with it, that she never appreciated enough its rare splendour.

There was so much else around me too. Other peaks beckoned me toward them and dense foliage glimmered in a state both here and not here, known and not known. When I finally sat down at the summit with a book of poems open on my lap, wildflowers like arctic avens split through the earth beside me. They were, it seemed, unbothered by the encroaching winter season: resilient, determined, unwilling to go.

*

The summer right before I left for Scotland, I climbed Assiniboine as part of a multi-day hike with a small group of friends. At 3,616 metres above sea level, it is the tallest mountain in the southern region of the Rockies. Five years later, as I climbed the modest ascent of Sleeping Buffalo, these two mountainous timelines of my past coalesced: smallest and tallest fusing together in an ephemeral state of memory. It was there, in Banff, looking outward at a world that I had become a stranger to, riven with elk and spruce and larch, that I realised Assiniboine had been my send-off. I didn't know it back then, but that climb – long, arduous and magnificent – was how I said goodbye to the mountains and to the landscape of Alberta. To the beautiful terrain that had taught me so much about myself and my desires as a young woman.

I remember looking past the open tent flap and seeing, through the diamond of that window, Mount Assiniboine layered in snow. The soft evening sky with its powdery clouds lurked, silent and searching, behind the salient foothold of that tall peak. Other tents filled with other blissfully tired and aching hikers were scattered around us. But we were angled just so, positioned in a way that let us feel remarkably alone in our reverence. I peered out from within the tent's margins, enclaved by green nylon that was torn and duct-taped in some places. It harboured signs of the many forested journeys I had taken thus far in my life and have not taken again since. From there, the pyramidal shape of Assiniboine was all I could see. It was, for that brief moment, all my heart had space to know.

*

Why did I want so badly to leave? Why only now that I'm gone does Alberta's beauty leak into everything I write? For so long, I couldn't wait to get away from my home province, from its slush and snow, from the endless flatlands of the interior plains and the sense of loneliness that flared within me every time I looked outside. Now, a quiet tenderness for these landscapes creeps up over me with regularity. These are places I no longer know in the same way as before. They are an ever-changing collection of impressions.

In Banff – as a visitor, a stranger, an unfamiliar – something in me ached. It was a feeling of grief even the mountains could not quieten. I think now of my ancestors who left India, of my parents who left East Africa, and of my own leaving of Canada. It strikes me how migration, a movement so easily posed as linear, as to and from, is in fact recursive. Migration is an act of weaving: a back and forth of multiplicity that forever repeats itself, erasing and accumulating in turn.

The years away deepen continuously and will, soon I think, become unquantifiable. The mountains underscore my memory and sense of self. I wonder if this is how it always is and always will be. I wonder if leaving is the thing that will always prompt love.

48.0905° N, 11.4030° E

Marvellous Things: Women in the Forest

It is a blustery winter evening and trees glower from the shadows of Stockdorf, Germany. There is a sheen to them, a wet and slippery glistening. It had rained all morning and when we finally venture out, the clouds are drizzling lightly still. I flip up my hood so it covers my eyes.

My friend L and I, and her small son, are going for a walk in the nearby forest in the dark. It is only just after 5 p.m., but the days are short in December and light wanes quickly. I have been noticing time differently here. It moves according to L's son and her own vast and varied responsibilities as a new mother. We bundle him up, bleary still from his nap, and put him in his stroller, the three of us seeking out this adventure together. I feel a small thrill as we leave the warmth of our temporary home. There is a wide expanse of possibility unfurling before us. The dim streets and their quietness hold the suggestion of the unknown, a shape that I find myself eager to explore.

The evening deepens and we watch as the world around us transforms. The dark is disorienting, especially in an unfamiliar place. The waymarkers we had locked in our mind's eye during the day dissolve into slick black roads and buildings that barely creep out from their murky shadows. There is a giant house on the corner of the street that is almost entirely made out of glass with all its lights on, and it begs us to look inside, to peek in and see with clarity the lives of those who live there. I feel watched and watchful, alone and not alone. We are only at the cusp of leaving and I know already that this walk is not something I would have done by myself. I sense this is the kind of night that will subvert expectations. The kind that needs an accomplice. Darkness closes around us in full as we head onto old paths made new by bewilderment.

*

In Edinburgh, I live a somewhat lonely life. I know it takes years, perhaps close to a lifetime, to find footing in a new place. Even after eight years, I feel like I'm not quite there yet. I am adrift and my love for the city is cleaved with homesickness for my past lives. Often, for days at a time, I retreat into myself and speak to no one. Friendship feels as slippery as the rain-slick greenery around me now. I miss not only the land on which I had sown iterations of my life – the prairies and mountains and Pacific coastline – but also the people held within the shoals of its memories.

A few months ago, when L and her partner, two of our best friends, invited T and me to Stockdorf for a visit over the winter, we agreed immediately. I had been drawn to the prospect of reuniting with them. It felt like a step toward overcoming the reclusive attitude I had slowly been forming like a bad habit.

Friendships have ebbed and flowed over my lifetime, and I have become comfortable with the alternating distances and closenesses of them. But recently, there is a palpable shroud of loneliness creeping over me that feels different to the natural rivering of adult relationships. It is noticeably affecting me and my sense of being in the world. I feel like I am losing perspective, suspended in the unsatisfying gels of a digital existence that furiously feeds my alienation. In *BFFs*, writer and editor Anahit Behrooz writes that 'friendship is, and has always been, a physical proposition, a corporeal act that occurs between people'. I feel like I don't and can't know my own heart without the reciprocity of friendship in its most physical, tangible form. Without this proximity, I slip out of and away from myself.

In Stockdorf, I find shelter for my body in others. I share space with people I love who are also from Canada, a homeland that holds me still, even if I worry that grip is becoming a ghostly one. And the comfort I find prompts me to make a promise to myself. I want to be present with the people I know in my current home in the same way. In a way that is embodied and slow and woven with care.

*

The sky is indigo and I can feel the air growing colder. It is our last day in Germany but our first time really seeing Stockdorf, having opted instead to take the twenty-minute train ride into Munich in days past. Tasks of domesticity and the exuberant Christmas markets kept us busy for most of our time together, but now a hush falls over us. Before our travels, it had been almost a year since I had seen L and, in this stillness, I feel it. An opening that beckons our minds to roam freely. This is a stretch of time we can settle into and spend remembering who we are to each other.

In the dark, an expansive forest and its full chamber of trees look almost like any cluster of foliage pressing forth from the shadows. We find ourselves on a deserted pavement along an unknown street and peer tentatively into every gathering of trees we encounter. Along the wet and shimmering roads, everything begins to look uncanny, and I start to feel unnerved.

In *Two Trees Make a Forest*, Jessica J. Lee considers how the wood radical forms part of the Chinese characters of her first name, writing, 'I find a quiet ease in the notion that forests can be built into who we are.' I think L and I both have a deep love for forests, and our lineage is that of the captivating northern terrain in Alberta. In fact, much of our early friendship was formed while walking amidst the wintery treelines of its mountains and foothills, learning about the margins of our bodies while entwined in evergreen landscapes. Forests are built into who we are and into the foundations of our friendship. This evening, during our precious time together, we are determined. From our cursory research earlier that day, we decide that the forest is snaking all around us from multiple directions and we continue on.

When we finally arrive at the path, the stroller making its way down bumpy roads, I see that it's completely veiled by the night sky. There are no lights at all, only a trail barely visible between a passageway of trees that loom over us, dark sutures against the dark sky.

*

I grew up with the mythology that forests are ominous places, places to get lost in, or places to house a cautionary and didactic tale. And even tonight, the draw of the forest is both its illegibility and its tremendous wonder. The trees, fractal-like and knowing, have an ability to conceal, to 'keep a secret' like the poet Carl Phillips writes in his meditation, 'Among the Trees'. As we enter, and then disappear into the forest, I think about our visibility. I wonder if anyone can see us and, if so, what they might be thinking. We are two young women with a baby, chatting in a language that isn't German, our foreignness amplified by our very proximity to one another.

In Edinburgh, I know which darkened alleyways I would consider walking down at night, but in Stockdorf, I'm unsure. I know this forest, so close to an array of family homes in a quaint neighbourhood, poses no real danger. Still, a tentative feeling washes over me. This isn't the first time on our short trip together that I find myself thinking about how few brown women I have seen so far in this part of Germany. It isn't the first time, either, that I find myself thinking about how few brown women I see in forests at all. If anyone is watching us, our soft silhouettes vanishing into the eclipse of trees, I wonder how quickly they will think to themselves that I don't belong.

As if she has sensed my feelings, L asks if I'm more afraid of encountering an animal or a human in the darkness. Almost without hesitation, I reply, *human*. It's reflexive and not entirely true, but in that moment, as these latent feelings of difference hum under my skin, it's authentic. I think about the myth of Daphne, the nymph who transformed herself into a tree, who became the forest itself, to escape the violence of men.

But the foreboding nature of the forest lies, too, in its more-than-human inhabitants. I am afraid of big animals like wolves and bears, something that made itself known to me while camping last summer at Emerald Lake in the Pacific Northwest. There, I had found it hard to sleep in my backpacking tent after seeing a golden black bear running through the field directly across from my campsite. That same night, one of the nearby campers told me a story of how once, when he was utterly alone, a small herd of wild elk circled his tent early in the morning while he was inside. Wild animals can be aggressive and unpredictable, especially in the isolated areas backpackers are most drawn to. All night during a fitful sleep, I dreamed of the furred creature waiting for me just beyond the tent's opening.

*

The strange and wonderful forest is a portal. Manoeuvring the stroller with us down a rocky but pleasantly wide trail, L and I press on until it feels like we are within the depths of the shadowland. As we pass through, I sense a change in energy. It's as if we have crossed into a new narrative formed by the fringes of dark trees, and I find myself giddy. The forest and the darkness, especially together, feel forbidden. So often in writing workshops and classes, I ask my students to think about how they feel in nature, and invariably, discussions about women feeling unsafe when alone in wild or rural spaces come up. I think that the very responsible version of myself wouldn't go further—

And yet, there is this version of me. The other self, with all my flaws and impulses. The woman who finds the walk mystical and enchanting and is enamoured with this different look at the forest she would not have had otherwise. Here is a forest I realise I will likely never visit again. I wonder how to memorialise this landscape that I cannot see, which still pulls me in.

Slowly, my eyes adjust to the starlight and I view the blurred treescape with wonder. I observe that the deciduous trees have long lost their leaves and stick out bare branches in a way that chimes with the gothic novels I am obsessed with. My first and most beloved copy of *Wuthering Heights* had a staunch, naked tree on its cover, its branches becoming creased and worn with each reread. In those novels, too, the ones I especially love, the forested landscapes often mimic the psychology of unruly women characters. Those who leaked outside the societal expectations that tried to contain them. Women who transgressed.

In his essay, Carl Phillips writes that 'woods and forests have long been a queer space', a place to explore one's sexuality. A forest provides a 'natural context for sexual intimacy', he continues, and this can give, 'if not a sense of wholesomeness exactly, then a sense of permission, at least, to what can feel like – what we've been made to feel *is* – transgression'. There is an alluring kind of privacy within forests. They extend us an invitation to unearth ourselves and our creatureliness outside of the boxes that confine us.

My body disobeys many societal expectations. My queerness has, over the course of my life, felt like one of them. This is especially because it is often perceived as at odds with my Muslim identity. Now I think back to one of my early coming-out moments, where a small group of friends and I had sat across from a view of the mountains at sunset. We were in Banff National Park, surrounded by montane forests, and I had felt that inarticulable feeling of the sublime – that utter serenity and unabashed freedom that comes with being in nature at the right time in one's life, with the right people. In times of self-isolation, it becomes possible to hide the truth from oneself. But there was something about those trees, about how they arced over me to create a protected space, that opened a valve within me. It's difficult, I realise now, not to feel close to others, not to want to divulge secrets in order to cultivate closeness, within an intimate circlet of trees. Within their wooded sanctuary.

*

The trees are spindly and reaching, and they look like they don't belong in real life. I can see only their silhouettes and, to me, the towering trunks with gaps below and some density up high look like pine trees. L says that when she got off the train on the night she arrived in Stockdorf she thought she smelled pine. I think of how we urge forward all of our senses in order to make sense of the night.

There is also a thicker shape: not pine, but something more like the spruce or fir I always see on my visits home to Alberta. These guard the path at the outskirts of the trail, looking important under the effervescent glow of our newly lit phone torches. It seems like we stand still forever, watching, time changing its scales yet again. The tallest of the trees settle sweetly in the sky above us, haloed by a luminous cloud.

I snap photographs of the trees and the impenetrable darkness between them, trying to capture some of the evening's truth: the way it is so haunting and eerie, this forest. And how it feels so strangely special and enthralling to be there, to walk next to a friend who I find myself being honest with, as if the darkness, as if being unseen, allows for the taboo of confession. There is little else to rely on but each other. And in this forest, even in moments of silence, there is the deep sense of togetherness. This is a shared experience, a binding of our bodies as they are hugged within a chamber of trees.

*

When I was nine years old, my childhood best friend K and I used to sneak away from school and spend our lunch hour in a ravine near our primary school. I have vivid memories of crossing the threshold into all that green, into the nourished forest: soft ground under my feet, wind billowing hard against our small bodies – just a little brisker than at the playground – and the urgent, rushing sound of moving water some way into the entrance of the trees.

There was something numinous and exhilarating about leaving our playground and classroom behind. What drew us in almost as much as the forest itself was knowing that we were participating in something just outside of the boundaries. Forests are 'strange and wonderful places', writes novelist Sara Maitland in *Gossip from the Forest*. They hold 'a sense of enchantment and magic, which is at the same time fraught with fear'. We knew we were breaking the rules and letting our bodies move toward something we loved, easily propelled by our own agency.

I know, also, that this is a violation I would not have dared to assume alone, that the enchantment and hold of the trees was made more significant by our friendship, our togetherness. It was an experience on the peripheries of something possibly dangerous, and it locked our small hearts to one another. Being in that forest together, at that young age, felt like being part of a glittering folk tale. That ravine was part of our coming of age; our draw to it was symbolic of all that we wanted to escape from in our lives. The hardships that we couldn't quite articulate as children but felt deeply in shape-shifting bodies.

I think about this ravine a lot, even though I know it is constantly transformed through my own remembrance and retelling. Part of me believes I'm so drawn to writing and remembering it, this sidelong forest, because it is a site of possibility not born entirely from imagination. The charm of this dreamlike memory is the realness at its core. I both shed and accumulated in that space. Every time I entered the forest, I remember I had to swallow my fear until it became a tiny seed, unretrievable from the overgrowth of young excitement. In my memory, this forest is a place of growing up, of understanding girlhood and young friendship and of learning, for the first time, to trust.

In her study of novels by Mahasweta Devi, the scholar and literary critic Jennifer Wenzel calls the forest *a room of one's own*, a place of peace and solitude where one can be alone with time to think one's own thoughts. I wonder if that's what draws L and me deeper into the forest now, and if it's what drew us both into all the other forests we've walked together in the past. Likewise, I wonder if that space to explore, to become, was what drew K and me into the ravine as girls, the trees acting as cyphers for those formative years.

*

L and I decide that we will only walk until we can no longer see the lights behind us, but that moment comes and goes. A gentle snowfall begins, only visible in the shard of light offered by our phones. Up ahead, we see what looks like another road. Her son moves around in his stroller, the only sound beside our talking, our sharing of our private and inner lives with one another. There in that mostly unseen forest, we speak so much about womanhood and the shadow labour involved, especially for L as a new mother. She says that if her son wasn't so fidgety, we could have walked further, perhaps up to the road, perhaps even crossing its borders, moving beyond that gateway into another place even further from what we know.

But he becomes more discontent, and she thinks maybe he is growing bored of the dark. We wonder if it reminds him of the ritual of napping and the feeling of being ready to wake. Or maybe he is restless because most of his days are spent arrested by the new shapes and colours he is encountering as he sees more of the world, all of which now remain hidden behind the veil of the night.

To me, the secluded evening forest trail, where we are surrounded by darkness and a softly falling snow, feels unbearably profound – like we are witches performing a ritual. We are two women rediscovering ourselves, in some small way, amidst the scent of pine in a forest so dark and dismantling that I hadn't even bothered looking for the moon, nor did I see it now in the pitch-blackness. I find myself smiling at the sweetness of how this moment that so utterly moves me, that feels excitingly like trespass, that pulls me back into the whimsy of girlhood, is for L's son, a small and possibly boring experience.

I am left enchanted by the forest's innumerable secrets. But he is only just a year old and doesn't yet know the marvels of absence and elision. He has yet to feel the flutters propelled by a hidden thing, like the magic of a treeline that isn't visibly there, but which exists in manifold through the forest fictions you collect as you age.

54.1165° N, 111.9213° W

Haloed pines

'It is there, in the neighbourhood of experience, that my childhood home is nowhere to be found.'

— Billy-Ray Belcourt

In my older sibling's house, most of the windows point southeast and out toward a vast snow-covered grassland that stretches out as far as I can see. She lives at the edge of the city. We drive through Edmonton until the cars on the road dwindle and the streetlamps become further and further apart. Because of the entwining highways across the province, it's close enough for her to get to work downtown while also being a relatively affordable and picturesque area where she can raise my two nephews. I love visiting her home and looking out into the distance behind it. Every so often, a new build or a construction site interrupts the flat landscape, but not as often as I expect. The view feels to me quintessentially Albertan: unyielding flatlands beneath a gorgeous and animated sky, several feet of untouched snow and, occasionally, near-zero-visibility fog which goes ahead and erases all of it. Her home is part of a sprawling, busy city that continuously spills out of its loose margins.

At her kitchen table one evening, my two sisters and I eat dinner while squabbling about our memories, our voices rising to overtake one another's, each of us correcting what is false or misremembered. We are disagreeing fervently over certain periods of time in our lives – who slept where, who was present for what – and frowning in exasperation when we don't get our way, two against one. This kind of camaraderie is not unusual for us; our relationships with one another are slightly different depending on what topic we're discussing and who is closer in age or in geographical proximity. I'm visiting over the holidays from Edinburgh, so I'm the furthest away. But I'm also the middle sister and sometimes I can offer a generational bridge between the other two.

In my art, I write about our lives and our family all the time. In fact, tonight our conversation springs from my offer to revisit Vilna together, the small town in northern Alberta where we all lived for two years when I was ten years old. Vilna is a place tied so closely with our childhood traumas, on the scales of both familial fracturing and political strife. I've written so much about it in recent years through the lens of nostalgia, from a reimagining of the past, and I want to see it again outside of the mythos I have created. I feel like my sisters are an integral part of the story as it exists in my mind and as I might remake it; their anecdotes and memories conflict with my own, but gently, like plumes of smoke coming together.

Subjectivity grounds my work, so even within my own experiences, I know this kind of historicising is firstly a creative act. One of my favourite essays to teach is 'Evidence, in Track Changes' by Jennifer Lunden, where she publishes not only her essay, but also her mother's annotations and comments alongside it. On the sidebar are notes like: 'I don't remember it that way' and 'I want to protest: This is not true! But I may have a faint memory of it.' I think of where, in my reminiscing about Vilna, my sisters might mark up my document with contradictions, or where they would similarly reflect on their own feelings of alienation and discomfort during those years. In *Another Way to Split Water*, my first collection of poems, I wrote about Vilna underneath the shroud of metaphor and abstraction without naming the town itself. But both of my sisters could pinpoint immediately what I referred to, even when the lens of my writing pointedly looked away; this makes the poetry and its hidden traumas feel less lonely. It makes my experiences feel more robust, full and real.

There's also a new urgency to our remembering. We often think about our childhoods together, but lately we have been doing so more often and more deliberately. I've fantasised about revisiting Vilna many times before, but I've never taken any real steps to make it happen until now. I think this has to do with the progression of our father's illness over the last six months, which has prompted a kind of purposeful reflection, a keen nostalgia, and maybe a need to try and understand, even retrospectively, the decisions he made over the course of our lives.

Still, I was surprised at how eager the two of them were to visit that small northern town as well, how readily they agreed to come with me on this strange trip to recover my missing memories of a place that rears away from clear recollection. Right now, it's too dark to see the snow and fields just outside the kitchen window, but I imagine they are a preview of the long drive we'll take together through the prairies in a few days' time.

—

When I look back to those childhood years, it's the drive from Edmonton to Vilna that I remember the most. I'm always drawn back in time to that evening when we first moved, when we packed our belongings into our van and shut its door on our former life. In my mind's eye, I can see with certain clarity the long stretches of prairies, the highway lines lodged in-between an unending flatness with wheat grasses, needle-and-thread and acacia shrubs on either side.

But even within that sharp imagery, my memory falters. The digital map says one thing, while my visions of the past say another. The drive is just under two hours, not a full three. The route is northeast rather than a single sharp line northward. This pixelated truth makes me uneasy. What else am I misremembering? Back then, we as a family documented so little, and whatever tangible artefacts once existed have since been lost. To map our old route now is a peculiar meeting of the past and present, a coalescence of timelines. My long adult arm reaches back into the experience of childhood and tries to make sense of what glistens there.

That first night, as we drove alongside Alberta's swathes of golden canola fields, I squinted against the evening light and tried to imagine the life that waited for me. Outside my window, the prairies opened like an outstretched palm, forming a permanent flatline that tricked me into believing time had stopped. I sometimes spotted the towering silhouettes of finely clustered trees along the highway. They were coniferous, likely a type of spruce or pine, and I traced blue cone after blue cone as we travelled straight ahead into what I perceived as nothingness. I didn't know, then, the nuances that separated flatness from emptiness, the awesome living quality of these landscapes' infinite space.

In the days leading up to our move, Vilna had become a place interwoven with fiction. The decision to pick up our lives and leave Edmonton happened very quickly, a plan forged by my father who was developing a pattern of seeking out new business ventures with startling frequency. Convincing a family to leave the deepened grooves of its life was not an easy task. Though I couldn't discern my mother's feelings, I knew that my sisters and I dreaded the move. Reena was six years older than me, approaching womanhood, and I understood even then that her losses would surpass my own. As if to quell our anxieties, my parents would tell us iridescent tales about what to expect. But my mother had only seen the town once before, on a fleeting visit, and my father's tendency to exaggerate left us feeling ambivalent.

Like many small midwestern towns, Vilna laid claim to one of the 'world's largest' attractions. This fascination with giant novelty objects was evident all over the province, with more than a hundred of them scattered across the prairies. Oversized replicas of the ordinary and everyday were strategic marketing tools, and my parents seemed to understand this. Vilna's claim to fame was a six-metre-tall cluster of mushrooms, and they tried their hardest to market this attraction to us.

When my mother would tell me Vilna has the 'world's largest mushroom', I didn't know what to imagine. She couldn't really explain it either and I realised our family was perfectly removed from this tradition of roadside novelty attractions. The custom of it, the North American fascination with big things, escaped us totally. Neither of my parents grew up solely in large cities, but small-town Alberta and the rural villages of Tanzania don't have this tradition in common. All along that first drive, I imagined, instead, organic matter – giant mushrooms alive in a huge field and grown too big and unruly to be kept in the supermarket. Eventually, the giant mushroom became a joke between us all.

Though it's now in a landfill somewhere in Edmonton, the night we first arrived in that small town as children, the three of us lined up in front of the tall statue for an obligatory photograph. I remember the lights around us were broken or else turned off, and the replica of three brown mushrooms loomed uneasily in the dark; they were hardly visible beneath the canopy of stars. Today, I can only imagine the glow of our hesitant smiles under the flash of a disposable camera.

—

Moving from Edmonton to Vilna was the first time I had to learn what it means to physically leave a home behind and tuck myself into the imagination of a new place: the strong, archetypal, rural Albertan narrative that existed long before we arrived. This, I know now, was a depiction of the western prairies that was consciously constructed by settlers in the mid-nineteenth century. It was a rendering geared toward British settlement of the region and its subsequent control. Historical records and curricula about the prairies existed within the framework of settler-colonialism. They violently omitted the faces and lives of Indigenous people in the area, or otherwise cast them into the periphery beneath the confines of the European gaze. The resulting narrative of this region steadily became one of whiteness and imperialism, though as a child I only grasped this through feelings of uncertainty and discomfort.

The feminist writer and independent scholar Sara Ahmed writes that 'strangers are not simply those who are not known in this dwelling, but those who are, in their very proximity, already recognised as not belonging, as being out of place'. A family like ours didn't exist in the mainstream repository of history and literature about Canada's rural spaces. In this landscape, not the natural world more broadly, but the cultivated landscapes erected by settler-colonialism, landscapes where difference and alienation were primarily responses to sites of whiteness, we were embodied others. The backdrop of rolling farmlands had carved out their resolute identity without my family's nebulous pattern of migration in mind, and this identity was fundamentally at odds with our lives as South Asian Muslim immigrants.

It was at this point in my life that I was beginning to understand the limits and assumptions placed on my body by others. My budding recognition of race began in my early school years, but I felt the tensions of femininity and Western expectations of beauty gnaw at me as well. Those pains linger even now. I'm riddled with past attempts at trying to meet unattainable standards that, rationally, I know are buttressed by whiteness and misogyny. But my desire to be beautiful within those narrow confines is reflexive still. It's a desire that has been developed over a lifetime and followed by disappointment that, instinctively, I brace myself for.

Still, at ten years old I was not yet aware of uprooting and its harshness, and I stared uneasily ahead at the unfurling provincial road to my new life. I didn't know how my body would fit in or be welcomed in the countryside, or if it would be welcomed at all. With the twilight landscape blurring outside our moving window, I participated in an act of leaving that wasn't an inherited migration for the first time. My inherited past, an inheritance that entangled with barely conceivable Tanzanian landscapes, was only just starting to film over my perspective at such a young age. With this latest move, I was becoming a palimpsest of displacement layered with eras of different longings.

The act of leaving is two-pronged. It involves tumbling forward toward the future, an unyielding momentum that at times can feel like an adventure. But it also lays bare the past. To leave one's home generates a new category of ephemeral possessions: all the things left behind. I close my eyes and try to identify what I could have been feeling at such a major juncture of my childhood. I think I understand that this drive and what it represents was the very first rupture of selfhood. Before then, I couldn't have understood what it meant to remember a home, to look back and feel the well of complicated emotion that comes with such a specific kind of nostalgia.

On that journey, with no large trees or houses to catch and hold the unending dark sky, I realise it was beginning to gather: the start of a questioning I would return to and scrutinise for the rest of my life. That strange methodology of documentation that mimicked the inexorable horizon above the prairies, relentless and steadfast. My unwillingness to let go of the earliest walls that first held up a life, an obsession that will never leave me.

—

Our ancestries haunt us and it is impossible not to witness their shape-shifting griefs. I have spent a lifetime doting over the distant past, ruminating on the cartography of bodies that resemble my own but came long before mine. I have spent hours contemplating a lineage that flows like a river across a fluctuating map of a different world. In *Unbearable Splendor*, Sun Yung Shin graphs migration as a star and weaves together her own reflections on diaspora with texts from NASA Science. She quotes that 'when a massive star dies, it leaves behind a small, dense remnant core', prompting the question: what is the remnant core that is left behind during acts of migration? What is the uncanny or imperceptible material – often manifested as silence – that glides or trembles underneath a life?

I once read an article that suggests our childhood homes haunt us too, and that this haunting might never stop. When moving across national borders, there are certain social, historical and political realities that underscore future lived experiences. But there are other borders that we cross perhaps more quietly, those that exist between urban and rural spaces, between densely populated cities and rolling farmlands, between neighbourhoods, sometimes right next to one another, that are segregated by affluency and class. There are even the illusive borders between time: childhood, young adulthood, womanhood, that we river through, sometimes without noticing exactly what changes in-between. These boundaries mark not only our remembered ancestries but also our own changed identities over time. Remnant cores are left behind as we sweep across these borderlines, too.

On the morning my sisters and I are to drive to Vilna and see it again after twenty years, I am bleary-eyed and tired, wrung with nervous anticipation. My mother's home is quiet, the silky sky still dark outside the living-room window. This city exists as I always remember it, as I most intimately know it: held in silence and gripped by an icy winter. It's half past six in the morning, which is the latest I have woken up since arriving here. I have been in Edmonton for almost two weeks and my jet lag is only settling now, just in time for me to return to Scotland again in a few days.

I'm not sure what will come of this crossing: the meeting of past and present, the confluence of spaces and timelines born from contradictions. This is a different kind of hybridity that emerges not from the striations of an imagined ancestral homeland, but from the real memories of a place I left behind. We are pulling on a tender thread, tugging at the hearts of our young selves. I want it to be significant, for the long drive across acres of snow to mean something, to fix something, to reveal something about who we were and, subsequently, who we became. I want my searching to coalesce and catch like a beautiful poem, epiphanic and revelatory.

In *Northern Light*, writer and academic Kazim Ali revisits his own childhood home in Manitoba, in a different small town in the Canadian prairies, and though his travels are brief, he unearths a new and transformative understanding about the environment. Still, I know that revisiting Vilna for a single day, a town which has certainly changed since I lived there, can only have a limited impact on my understanding of time and place and community. I try to tamp down my expectations. And as I dress in my warmest clothes, preparing for the brisk northern cold that I remember, I think, *I am older now*. The self I am today is, for the most part, the self I have chosen. I can look back with compassion. I am harbouring a soul that wants to – and can – empathise with the wayward path that eventually brought me here, to the person I am.

When she arrives to pick me up, Reena is wearing a cropped fleece jacket, a thin barrier against the late December weather. I lend her my scarf and an extra layer, and then we're on our way to pick up our younger sister, Shazna, from the outskirts of Edmonton where she now lives with her fiancé and two cats. The car ride echoes both with our reminiscing and with an early 2000s playlist, another way we dig ourselves into the trenches of the past. We scream-sing old R&B hits with the sun streaming through the car windows. I love the prairie skies, always unabashed with colour and light. Every day that I've been back, I've pointed up at the sky at least once and said to whoever was listening, *look at how beautiful the light is*. And every winter I visit home is marked by at least one remarkably bright magenta sunrise, as if the world, for a few brief moments, is aflame.

—

The past exists in flashes and misrememberings, always ebbing just beyond my reach. But there are some memories that I think I can grasp, like small tethers binding me to the grasslands of my past. I remember Vilna had a Main Street. It was lined with a few shops – one of everything. One grocery store, one hardware store, one place to get ice cream, one place to rent videos. That was also where my parents' restaurant was, the business venture that was the main and perhaps only motivation for this sudden relocation. I could walk to it from our home by crossing one long alleyway interspersed with mobile homes and often slick with dangerous black ice in the winters.

An adjoining door connected my parents' restaurant, which my father named Vilna Café, to the neighbouring bar. This door was behind the counter where we kept the cash register and adjacent to the doorless entrance to our restaurant's industrial kitchen. My parents could swing from one building to the next easily. My mother would slip into the kitchen one moment and then disappear behind the bar door the next. I remember her then-long curly hair linking with the ringlets of smoke that would emerge from the darkness of that room. It was there I would see a brief glimpse into her life, flashes of someone who was not just my mother, but still, then, a young woman. Only a few years older than me now, I realise, as I write this.

What does she think about her time in Vilna? From the threads of what I can remember of her small-town life, my mother was a woman drifting, too, away from her religion. On one of our recent video calls, where I caught her at work clad in her dark green uniform and blue wire-framed glasses, we ended up reminiscing about the past. This is unusual for us. When I was young, my mother was an urn filled with secrets, and I rarely got a look inside. I don't think this unfurling is purely because I've started asking the right questions; rather, I think the silence of womanhood has loosened as I've got older and the shared traumas between us have made themselves known. It's difficult not to take them all and try to translate them in my art as a way of processing. I'm teaching myself to both uncover the mystery and let it go.

She recalled that time with laughter. And she revealed in an impish voice that those years – the strange, lambent memories she has of Vilna – were her wild years. My mother married at eighteen and had her first child at nineteen. Her life was quickly moored to us, her three daughters. After so much cultural and social obedience, it was that small rural town that gave her a chance to explore life beyond motherhood. There was such immense isolation and loneliness there, and for better or worse, that lack of connection to past lives and people allowed her to reinvent herself.

Her wild years. I laughed too. This was a joke and it was an admission. It was as mischievous as it was knowing. And as an adult, I understand it. I have spent my whole life leaving places and reinventing myself. I have spent my whole life running away from hurt and toward a stronger self that I will never catch up to.

—

When I think about past drives between Edmonton and Vilna, they always take place in the dark. I know this is a trick of my memory. Layers of recollection interpolate; they ultimately fit into a shape I can quickly turn to, without having to think too deeply. A slowing darkness on either side of us. Headlights and moving shapes – elk, perhaps, but more likely cattle. The flickers of aspen and birch amongst the spruce trees, which, paradoxically, become more pronounced as the evening goes from blue to midnight. All that whitened bark. And many stars too, of course, but one in particular. The one that my father sometimes pointed to from his bedroom window. A bright, guiding flare in the sky.

For a long time, that drive was part of our routine: Vilna to Edmonton and then back again. Twenty years later, the day breaks and our drive takes place on a glaringly bright morning. This is only the first of many differences. As the city buildings disappear and we find ourselves on the highway, I feel momentarily surprised by how changed things look from my memory. There are unlatched trailers parked alongside the road with adverts spanning across them, and there are far fewer road signs than I recall. What I remember as vast and unending fields look compact and restrained next to the single-lane roads. Snowbanks creep up on each side of us, often swarming with winter birds pecking at the roadkill we see intermittently along our journey. Cattle meander around the farmland and there are horses fenced in, enfolded in rough blankets to keep warm.

Since I have left Alberta, there have been new initiatives to reintroduce wild bison to the prairies and other areas. We pass Elk

Island on our drive, where plains and wood bison engineer the ecosystem and shape the land. They graze near the highway, in areas allotted to them between cattle guards and other enclosures. Shazna loves to point them out. She notices them right away – their iconic shapes, their riveting musculature, the way they billow through grass or snow. It's through her that I learn about the wildlife in the northeast plains. I sense her affinity for the natural world, and it resembles my own. The two of us have braided ourselves with our adoration for nature, coming at it from different angles, from different places, at different times in our lives. Two sisters who, growing up, only ever imagined themselves as city girls, dislocated from rural life until forced to reckon with it.

We pass through the small town of Andrew and turn onto highway 45, where we see a coyote from afar before it runs across the road in front of us. Snapshots of a land I remember come back to me; the pines cascading out the window, haloed by the sun and beckoning us forward, so gorgeously corrugated with snow. The farmlands and fields with their spellbinding symmetry, rectangular patches of what I imagine are different crops blending together beneath the quilt of untouched snow. The first sign I see to Vilna informs us we are just over thirty kilometres away and as we get closer and closer to this small village that our lives have, in a way, always orbited around, I feel the first pangs of an emotion I can't exactly pinpoint.

The sun retreats into a muted blue sky that meets and intermingles at the horizon with the blue-tinged hue of snow. The monotone of sky and earth is disarming; it's as if we are suspended in a cloud. In this untethered space, it's easy to think of ourselves as moving backward. In a way we are, through the memories and stories we share with each other. The highway signs count down and I stare ahead, keeping my eyes on the tarmac as it cuts through the blended landscape.

Sometimes I wonder who I would be if we never moved to Vilna, I say. This is the question that is at the core of every childhood reflection. If not for this rupture, who would I have become? There is a sense of dissatisfaction in such a question, in the *what ifs* that linger behind it. I think of all the years I sluiced away to shame before I arrived at the person I am today, the person I feel happy enough with, but who slides quickly and relentlessly into her depression and self-doubt.

My sisters admit they wonder this about themselves too. We joke that we'd all be more well-adjusted, and then more seriously contemplate the different lives we may have led. We agree there are many things that would have been different: our sense of community at that young age, our religious identities, our parents' divorce – or so we think – and how they drifted away as life pulled them in various directions out of necessity.

—

In *Upstream*, Mary Oliver says, 'In the beginning I was so young and such a stranger to myself I hardly existed.' I only lived in Vilna for two years, and I wonder how much importance was retroactively placed onto such a fleeting experience. It wasn't just place, after all, that marked that time in my life. It was an entwined understanding: the multiplicity, the many threads of myself unravelling so that I could inspect each one closely. Perhaps more than anything, Vilna was like a funhouse mirror: a place wherein I was forced to see myself not accurately, but with the curves of misrecognition, a kind of bevelling shaped by another's gaze.

Every so often, I find myself researching answers to the question: *Where were you on 9/11?* In tens of thousands of historic online forum posts and articles, people recall where they were and what they felt when the Twin Towers fell. I think I'm fascinated with this question because it's one of my own clearest memories of Vilna in an otherwise empty field. I know where I was that day. I was a child in a classroom, watching the towers fall again and again on the repeated footage on the news. We watched this day play out on an old TV that had been wheeled into the classroom, a common detail I find in posts about that day; our gazes were fixed on it.

I should have said Vilna had one of *almost* everything, because it didn't have a mosque. This marked a strange schism in our way of life: a striking before and after. On one end of that timeline was my family's devout religious practice and on the other was our palpable alienation. We were hours away from our community. We were, unsurprisingly, given the demographic makeup of municipalities in rural Alberta, the only Muslim family in the vicinity.

In a post-9/11 context, especially in a small rural town in northern Alberta, the violent narrative of *them* versus *us* quickly unfurled. The safety of a nation and its character was defined by who fitted into its invented familiar space and who, in contrast, was the stranger. In *Black Skin, White Masks*, Frantz Fanon examines how another's gaze contributed to fixing his identity, how it was therefore defined by 'the white man, who had woven [him] out of a thousand details, anecdotes, stories'. In the wake of heightened Islamophobia at the turning point of 9/11, I witnessed my own strangeness unfold in the stories that emerged during these years, told by one neighbour to another.

Misrecognition seeped its way into my body; it instilled in me a profound and perpetually unfulfilled desire to be recognised, to be welcomed – a conflictual kind of belonging – in my environment. This desire, one I still have not completely shed, is a complicated one. It's a kind of belonging that has been criticised by scholars like Anita Chari and Glen Sean Coulthard, who argue that the politics of recognition is a flawed and problematic non-solution for structural injustice. After all, as argued by Chari, the discourse of recognition is 'dictated largely by the coloniser'.

It is during those formative childhood years that shades of love and loss and sadness begin to mature, to become more complicated, and I was starting to feel these emotions in suddenly personalised ways. I could sense my whimsy and vivacity becoming veined with the very beginnings of introspection and seriousness. This unsettled period of my life was, I think, the origin of my new, fierce quietness. And this distorted reflection, this turbulent understanding of self, became my truth for a long time.

In returning to Vilna, I find myself hoping I will retrieve something, some sense of childhood comfort, that I can retroactively feel as a ten-year-old girl. *Don't worry*, I tell that young version of myself. One day you will be able to put words to these sensations, and articulation will feel, even microcosmically, like liberation.

—

Across time and space, Vilna is increasingly caught in the slick, watery propulsions of memory. Each time I look back, my childhood becomes more and more fragmented, and remembering is like beachcombing for sea glass. I fear that, eventually, nothing real will wash onto shore. So I fuse the literal with the imagined in order to give expression to the child I was, the woman I am today, and all the selves in-between. I know this is a stopgap method against forgetting that allows me to reach back and walk into my childhood eyes.

Vilna is a place I haven't lived in or seen for twenty years. Even as we drive toward it, I am aware we will only grasp it briefly, shimmeringly. Etel Adnan opens her collection, *Shifting the Silence*, with lines that resonate with me now: 'The horizon's shimmering slows down all other perceptions. It reminds me of a childhood of emptiness which seems to have taken me near the beginnings of space and time.'

To imagine, talk or write about this small town, and its always shifting impression on me, keeps Vilna in a state of becoming. And perhaps, then, it is also in a state of 'becoming-homeland' – a homeland constantly in flux and ever-changing and thus impossible to easily slot myself into. A homeland with porous borders and no true origin, moving between past and future as if on a sliding scale. Every time I look back, every time I try to retrieve that now dark and faded memory of walking across a wide open farmer's field, or through the heavy door of that old restaurant, I take a different route through my imaginings. There are infinite ways to remember because I myself have since changed in infinite ways.

I access these memories indirectly, through back doors that allow me to circle the wounds I otherwise turn away from, the wounds that sting with familial conflict, loneliness and alienation, and especially with the harsh glare of Islamophobia after 9/11. My steps tread and retread images: the drive between cities, my mother's recollections, the stray tabby cat we nursed back to health and eventually took in, the vague shape of a northern lake I think I swam in, low winter sunshine and other disassociated snippets of a life. I peer through fog, smoke, blurred faces and evening shadows. I so rarely point my gaze toward what hurts directly, even though every image catches the light of my pain.

—

As I grow older, envious of the meticulous documentation and notes others keep, I linger in blank spaces more and more often. I slip into them, and the acknowledgement of purposeful forgetting is sharp and uncomfortable like touching a perpetually open wound.

Along with my missing memories, I also don't have any physical keepsakes. A few years after Vilna, when we were back in Edmonton, we moved house again. Perhaps it was disorganisation or stress or the inability to keep up with a life that seemed to be a road of constant hurdles, but my parents never were able to pack properly. In our hurried leaving, we left all of our memorabilia behind. All those sentimental stories, nostalgic possessions, old notes, photos of my mother's long hair, of my father's smile, of my grandfather, of our kitten Meenu, and home videos of birthday parties and Halloween costumes – all of it gone as if it never existed.

In *The Night Sky*, Ann Lauterbach writes: 'reality had no fixed address.' I know that even as I retrace my childhood, fiction remains fastened to a version of the truth, and that truth, too, is always moving in a liminal space of its own.

What happened here? I ask myself. I had spent so long running away and covering as much temporal and geographical distance from my past as I could, as if doing so would take me just out of reach of whatever trauma tried to follow me into the present. *I don't know.* I let go of that childhood version of myself a long time ago and I worry now that she's lost. No longer knowable. A figure of the past, who has been left uncherished and unloved. A young girl who fell into that open wound, lost to the fringes of the world.

When I first talked to my sisters about returning to Vilna, I think part of the reason I wanted to visit was to find her: that young girl counting her bismillahs while perched at the perimeter of her schoolyard. That young girl who housed each dua in her mouth and in her heart. That fleeting version of myself that I decided, after prolonged heartache, I couldn't live with anymore.

The person I was before I let others determine what and who was worthy of love.

—

As we approach Vilna, there bubbles up in all of us a strange and haunted sensation. Reena says she gets goose bumps as soon as we arrive. Shazna's expression is a mixture of discomfort and curiosity. In front of us, we see the laundromat that we used, the library and town hall that we spent so much time in, and the alley between our townhouse and Main Street that we would walk down every single day.

What shocks me the most is that none of us remember the building of our parents' restaurant and what it looks like. We have impressions: we remember big windows, we remember it was on the corner of the street, we even remember the inside somewhat clearly – spacious, with large dining tables around the perimeter and a drinks cooler on the far side. But as we glide into the town, past the *Welcome to Vilna!* sign Reena once painted as part of a summer job, and come up on the historic Main Street, we are, all three of us, disoriented. For some time, we sit in the car and face a series of buildings: the post office, the pool hall, Vilna Hotel (closed now), and a new cannabis shop called 'Good Times'.

We think that the restaurant might have become the cannabis shop, but it's Sunday and the shop is closed with the blinds drawn, so we can't see inside for confirmation. And anyway, to all three of us, that doesn't seem quite right. We know the restaurant was connected to a bar and this shop stands alone, unattached to the buildings on either side.

Could they have separated the buildings?

Did it used to connect to the pool hall – is that the bar we remember?

Neither of these options seem right, so we find ourselves heading to the back road behind Main Street.

How can we not remember?

Somehow, I can remember everything before Vilna.

I thought I would remember more.

Across the street is D & E Family Grocery. This, at least, looks exactly as I remember it, with the same ice-cream sign and ice machine propped outside the front door. We decide to go inside, both for the sake of our nostalgia and to see if anyone there might be able to tell us anything about what happened to the restaurant after our family left. We wander through the aisles, where I look for anything that might resemble a souvenir, then we head to the cash register to question the young employee.

He tells us he has lived in Vilna all his life, and when we ask if he knows anything about the restaurant, he tells us that it burned down some years ago. I feel my heart sink – I'm not sure why. Perhaps due to a latent attachment to an artefact of my history. Eventually, we find out he was talking about a different restaurant just outside of the village because, as it turns out, he is much too young to remember Vilna Café or what it became next.

We used to live here a long time ago, in 2001.

That's before my time.

At that, we laugh and are forced to confront how much we've aged since we lived in Vilna, and how long it actually took us to finally come back. For us, the prairies froze in time as soon as we left, but his words expose yet another frayed tether to this place that has moved on without us.

We're back in the car, on our way to revisit other landmarks like our childhood house, the local school and, of course, the emblematic six-metre-tall mushrooms, when our father calls. The young cashier couldn't answer our questions, but my father immediately knows. His welcome voice booms from the car's speaker. It's not the little closed shop; the restaurant was on the lower floor of the now run-down and permanently closed hotel, which is a giant, sturdy red building, with a row of large windows facing the street. Suddenly, it all clicks into place. Memories flood back and yes, that's right, the restaurant connected to the hotel bar – which it seems is still open and can be accessed through a side door. It's difficult to see inside through the concealed windows, but it all makes sense. *There* is the wall that separated the dining room from the kitchen. *There* are the steps we climbed every day to get inside. *There* it is, all of it, a ghostly version of what once was.

—

Will you write about living in Vilna as a positive experience? Reena asks at lunch afterward. We're grabbing pizza just outside of Edmonton, almost back in the porous city limits.

I tell her that I think so, but I can't be sure. After all, Vilna and especially the wide open space of the prairies are only symbolic, a marker of when things went wrong and not themselves the cause. Outside of our timeline, both these places exist and extend forward in time innocuously, and over the years I have learned to appreciate and perhaps even love them for what they are.

Those things in life that really hurt, calcified by years of distress and silence, I tend to leave out of my work. I am practising how to withhold from the creative expanse, because I am practising how to write for myself and not another's expectation. I don't want to share something that I'll later wish I could take back. I have done that before, when writing about my family too tellingly without their consent. I was a newer writer then, inexperienced with the world, unaware of how quickly an artist is asked to mine their life, and the lives of others, for content.

Because, Reena continues, *I don't think of it as a positive time in my life.* And there is that too. There are the dissatisfying truths, the stories that will write themselves into existence without closure and perhaps even resisting it. 'The act of questioning has to be its own reward,' says author Brandon Taylor, 'even as it promises to strip you of all your resolutions and coping mechanisms.'

Glancing back at the prairies in the rear-view mirror feels quietly profound. I accept that I am still the person I always was, riddled with the same questions and gaps that trail behind me wherever I go. There is peace in that acknowledgement.

Sometimes, there is no new and transformative meaning to be gleaned, no way of retroactively healing the children we were. Sometimes, there is only the sky bleeding into the snow, and blankness as far as the eye can see.

54.4597° N, 3.0244° W

Skin memories in Lake District mist

What was once clear becomes opaque. Five hundred million years of evolving rock faces, glaciated valleys, volcanic activity, river sediment and slender lakes roll underneath the mist. The thirteen valleys of the Lake District are stippled with ancient memories that meet new footfall. Imagine any beloved place under a lucent shroud and understand that uncertainty is its own kind of knowledge. That time and space are placeholder nouns for a migrating body. Here, the air is wet and cool. The fells are slick underfoot. I move in patterns determined by history, carved out by lava and ice sheets. All the while, the mist ebbs and flows but never burns off completely. The breath of water is its own record and I follow.

Like the quality of mist itself, like everything I write, my first memory of Grasmere oscillates between real and unreal, between one truth and another.

When I arrive, the sky is enmeshed in a discontinuous film of vapour. I think to myself: *I like this.* I like the way the atmosphere is suffused with tiny droplets. There is a kind of anonymity offered by this weather. The sky dispatches rivulet after rivulet of grey as far as I can see. The hazy cloud is sometimes thick, offering low visibility that intermittently disrupts my climb up Stone Arthur. Other times, it's a porous sheen draped over the fells. The scene in front of me is a veil, unable to decide whether it wants to stay mist or collect into a deep-set fog. It remains ghostly. In-between.

In *Strange Encounters*, Sara Ahmed writes that 'migration stories are skin memories: memories of different sensations that are felt on the skin'.

How does meaning change when I write about the sensations felt on my body amongst the white spruce in Canada versus the mangrove trees in Tanzania versus the silver birch in Scotland? How can the name of a place, of a tree in a particular place, carve out a luminous specificity that feels so much like the sensation of belonging? Ahmed continues:

> The physical sense of moving through space is enough to trigger a memory of another place. Memory hence works through the swelling and sweating of the skin.

'Skin memories' offer an explanation as to how I might hold multiplicity. They present a way to explore how I experience a range of different landscapes and provide me with a framework to better understand and care for my body. My presence in the natural world, my body existing within it unapologetically as a brown woman who flickers in and out of the mist – this is a way for me to take up space in all the places I'm from. The sensation of walking up Stone Arthur in the Lake District, condensation stippling on my skin, might trigger memories of moving through the heavy heat in Dar es Salaam, or walking through the stippling West Coast mist in Eugene, Oregon.

Further still, perhaps moving through mist in the Lake District triggers the inherited or ancestral memories that have been passed down to me through familial stories. When they find me, they swell into the shape of a body that came before mine.

I trail through the Cumbrian mist after an experienced hiker. Her artist biography describes her as a photographer and mountain leader, but I think I could also call her an ecologist. As we walk, she points out the scientific and common names of the plants around us. I learn about bracken, how it is an invasive species that covers at least 4 per cent of the Lake District.

The two of us are working on a collaboration. She is the director of a digital guidebook of writing prompts and experimental hiking routes in the Lake District. We are generating one of these routes as a pair. In her first email to me, sent via the contact form on my website, she said that she came across my name while researching *non-white writers who explore ecological issues*. I wonder at the words plugged into her search engine, the descriptions that lifelessly absorb or underscore my identity.

On our walk above Dove Cottage, best known for being William and Dorothy Wordsworth's Lake District home, we follow an ascending path up to Alcock Tarn. The ground below us is boggy, and my Scarpa hiking boots accumulate clods of mud that cause their grip to loosen. At regular intervals, panting heavily, I pause to look out at the fells.

I have watched my body change with critical eyes over the last few sedentary years. These years are crosshatched with grooves of anxiety and slurry griefs. I haven't yet found unconditional love for my body, which is a body that seeps out of so many societal expectations, but lately, I've been trying to show myself more care and gentleness. I find that, when walking, I appreciate my body in ways that elude me in my day-to-day life. I marvel at how it moves, how it looks under a gloss of sweat, and how it feels after a particularly challenging climb. In those ruddy, delirious interludes of exhaustion, I find myself giddy with gratitude for what my body can do.

As we climb further, the view is enveloped in an eddying haze. The mist tangles with mountain peaks and caresses the canopy of trees. The landscape seems to undulate in the grainy light and I'm mesmerised by its rippling.

I've lived alongside forests all my life, but as soon as I try to give the trees a name, they take on a kind of slippery strangeness. Even now, I might recognise the shape of one, attending to leaf textures and tree forks, but nomenclature drifts away. This tenuous hold on vocabulary makes me feel like an imposter, like there are specific rules to being in nature that I keep breaking. A real nature lover would *know*, wouldn't they? I sometimes worry I will show my cards and reveal that, for all my effort toward *decolonising nature writing*, I don't belong in these spaces after all. I'm afraid to admit that I'm perpetually catching up, trying to enter a conversation, an experience, that arranges itself without me in mind.

All of this underlines the darker feeling, too, that perhaps there is a desire to keep people like me out. Some bodies go through life without having to endlessly prove themselves, without having to prove their knowledge of green symbols.

I'm trying to understand why this act of naming feels so important to get right, and also why I just can't seem to match the sight of lobed leaves with a name – is it sessile oak?

At an event I once attended titled 'Landscape and Literary Culture', Aimee Nezhukumatathil said something along the lines of, *the trees don't ask you where you're from.*

As a young girl, I rarely imagined a body like mine, a brown woman's body, moving through the natural world. Now I spend time thinking back to the permeating images of whiteness, of wildness, I grew up with. There's so much that I've internalised about nature, about the transitory borders between 'natural' and 'urban', and where amongst those boundaries I'm placed by the white gaze. This feeling, which in essence is a feeling of erasure, makes me wonder about access to green spaces and which bodies are perceived as belonging within them.

Faces like mine are missing from the ecological archives. I wonder endlessly at what it means to 'belong' at all. I find myself wanting to uproot that word. I want to dissect its parts. I want to challenge its assumption of negative space.

Having only just met each other for the first time at Oxenholme train station, I expect to encounter some awkwardness with my companion. After all, we're alone on this experimental hike and we're basically strangers. Before we set off into the light rainfall, I even wonder if there might be more differences than similarities between us. This makes me realise that I am as guilty of making a set of assumptions about her as I fear she might have been about me.

When we arrive at Alcock Tarn, we are immediately greeted by a single Herdwick sheep, a breed endemic to the Cumbrian hillsides. The sheep is poised on a rocky outcrop, clear and resplendent in her place. Up here, the mist lessens incrementally, and I find myself enamoured by her round white head. My colleague smiles at me, and we both stop to take a photograph. After a few minutes, more sheep walk into our field of vision, trotting confidently up the rocky terrain.

Walking together is a way to unearth intimacy very quickly. The tarn is visible on our right, shards of grass spearing through its chilling water. Here, something *unclicks* between us, like the latch of a gate. Under the watchful gaze of the sheep, we begin, ourselves, to pour.

We share stories of our past selves with one another and the conversation grows animated, comfortable, friendly. At one point, she recalls an injury she had as a young person and we acknowledge how the layers and fissures of a body hold memory.

She says that the land holds memory too. I know this. But the reality of the words being spoken out loud as we imprint our steps into soil, participating in the recycled land memories that gather here, affects me in a sudden and unexpected way. My biology labs never mentioned this important quality of the earth: its way of freeing up our bodily space, of dislodging our anxieties and letting them disappear into a still, leafy November canopy.

There is a relationship between the natural world and the notion of homeland. I think of the ocean I have crossed to arrive at my current home in Scotland. The ocean crossings of my ancestors who migrated under colonial rule. The great sea of separation, the great sea of coming together. All the distances my body has travelled, distances seen and unseen, and all the imaginations I have metaphorised to seep through the borders. The word *endemic* lands in an unfamiliar rhythm on my tongue. I watch the Herdwick sheep and feel distress over my own untraceable lineage. I embody lifetimes of movement and migration. I can't even begin to grasp such a long, unbroken legacy.

My first memory of Grasmere is disorientation.

In Alberta, the fog was sometimes so thick there was near-zero visibility. It stalked the landscape, eliding the shape of trees, softening lodgepole pine into could-be willow. The anonymity offered comfort, but only to a point. Fog like this reduced a city into a series of indiscernible figures. It was a bewildering image, an altogether destabilising experience – how do you know where you are, or even who you are, without the ability to orient yourself?

In the Lake District, fog surrounds us with its imprecise brushstrokes, but the fog is only one fractal of my disorientation. As the cloud condenses, I am able to see only the silhouettes, the loping and obscure outlines of the fells. I can hardly see the body in front of me or my own limbs as I walk ahead, moving further into the escalating haze.

I'm no stranger to losing the particulars of my body. I know this kind of loss. It repeats and repeats, no matter how many ocean crossings to possible homelands. I let the fog obscure all of my historical and cultural and racial markers. This knowledge of how to make oneself small, so, so small, is the kind of knowledge I wish I never had.

I'm good at losing my body. I'm good at assimilating until I disappear.

We walk for hours and I record the shape of the Lake District as I learn it. Clouds caress the jagged hills. The ascent is slippery and my heart races. There is only trace sunlight between the gaps of trees. The sound of spilling water reminds me of my mother washing supermarket vegetables, liquid pooling in the sink like a small lake. The tarn reflects our faces back at us. And all the while, there is the mist. It riddles my notebooks with invitations – to pause, to think, to climb.

Between 1798 and 1803, Dorothy Wordsworth wrote her Grasmere Journals, where she catalogued her observations while walking in the Lake District. These field notes capture a dynamic landscape throughout the seasons. They are a literary heirloom answering the question: what do you remember about the earth?

In them, I look for excerpts about the mist and wonder if they resemble my own.

> We were afraid of being bewildered in the mists, till the darkness should overtake us. We were long before we knew that we were in the right track.

When I walk the loop above Grasmere over two centuries later, shrouded in the clouds of my own present tense, I become an echo of her echo. My poetry finds a hold in her language and I wonder, who will next write about the Lake District mist?

We stop every so often on the well-trodden pathway to write poetry. This is our effort to co-create with and within landscape. Our first writing prompt is inspired by poet Bhanu Kapil's *The Vertical Interrogation of Strangers*, a book that was recommended to me over a decade ago, after I lamented my own gap in knowledge of poetry written by South Asian women. Even as a South Asian woman myself, it sometimes felt impossible to retrieve such work back then, particularly given the pervading whiteness of the industry even within my own private writing circles. For me, the collection's long lines of imagination, how it associates and dissociates between continents, between voices, opened a world of possibility.

In the making of this book, Kapil travelled across the borders of India, the US and the UK, to interview exclusively women with South Asian heritage. The resulting collection brings together poeticised answers and reimagined experiences. It crosses space and silence.

At an early stop, maybe a kilometre away from the Rydal Water car park where we first began, I pause and write a response to one of Kapil's twelve interview questions: *what do you remember about the earth?* In doing so, I become an extension of the collection's many voices. I feel like paratext, material that exists outside of the main body of work, but which still pulses into meaning. I imagine all the other people like me who respond to Kapil in all these different ways. My writing is a tendril that cuts through the fog and joins their growing forest.

What is the collective noun for a group of brown women?

Chandra Frank writes that 'to be a Brown feminist is to forge connectivity through a chasm of difference'.

What do you remember about the earth? One woman asks and another answers, despite the long string of time between them, despite their different migration patterns. Despite the changing curvatures and ecotones and agencies across generations. Both body and landscape are dynamic, changing over time – ageing, eroding, evolving.

The path through Heron Pike swims in and out of view. We slip against the mud, momentarily frictionless. Our bodies rush dangerously forward, cascading like rainfall. For a brief second, even my companion is bewildered as we peer over and across the hills that stream with impermeable fog. Wet long grass becomes patterned with our confused steps: up and down, over and across, back and forth, until we finally familiarise ourselves again. A single distinct tree guides our way, its near-black branches stark against orange foliage and cloud-stricken skies.

In a brief moment on Nab Scar, I become the interstice of voices. My body and its own lived experience leak into the land's memory. I am here, making my own fleeting impressions. I come to understand a new version of myself through the shared languages of this landscape: one of soil, of bracken, of sessile oak. One of ghosts and in-betweens.

What do you remember about the earth?

Not so much the intersecting threads of insects, bracken, grass, fallen autumnal leaves. I remember the feel of the earth, damp and rich, against my skin. My skin is a palimpsest written with, first, ancestry, and then the scattering rain.

What I remember about the earth is stratified with skin memories, which are sometimes also gaps in historic knowledge. Memory and membrane come together in an act of cartography, where landmarks are written in forgotten first languages.

On this route that loops around Grasmere, the map I've created is layered with all the times I've walked away from the wind I know into an unfamiliar gale.

If my experiences unravel into a series of metaphors, of remembrances, then what does it mean to be present in nature when walking in a landscape? How can I pinpoint particularities on this moving, milky membrane of place? I pour and pour my feelings here, but the landscape remains steadfast throughout my questioning, my doubling. The trees don't ask me where I am from, but they do help me understand the answer to that question.

A metaphor for vanishing, for dissolving, for withholding, fog often finds its way into my poetry. A woman becomes the fog. An unanswered prayer is the fog. A body disappears into the fog. Fog is a way to make an object seemingly invisible, even when it is placed right in front of you.

I return to this image of fog in the Lake District, the ground cloud I must pass through. Particles lift and echo around me. The way forward is opaque. By continuing on, I have to trust the area's history, all those footsteps I walk into, as much as I have to trust the movement of my own body.

The world under a generous mist looks as if it is in the process of being erased. I think of all the trees I can and cannot name caught in the act of unbecoming or becoming one another. I'm ascending Stone Arthur on a wet November day, but couldn't I just as easily be walking through Alberta's ridge of Rocky Mountains? My body has its own muscle memory that calls back to those tall, Canadian peaks. One leg surges forward and remembers the climb up Assiniboine. There's the mix of stone and dirt and moss, the hard then soft pattern of my steps.

In a way, fog invites me into this landscape's loosened borders. My body responds to the familiar and the strange, retrieving contrasting skin memories as I allow myself in.

Route: Medium–difficult (13.5 kilometres, 2,970 feet of ascent).

Starting point: Rydal Water car park on the north side of the A591 between Grasmere and Ambleside.

This route climbs up to Alcock Tarn then descends again to the Greenhead Gill valley before climbing to Stone Arthur, Heron Pike and down to Nab Scar. For those who would like a less ambitious route, it's also possible to shorten the route by turning left (east) down the valley from Greenhead Gill to Michael's Fold and then following the path which traverses at a lower level, parallel to the A591, back to the original path above Town End. This alternative route is approximately five kilometres.

Accessible alternative: this route can straightforwardly be completed on any of the Miles Without Stiles routes.

Prompt: while completing the above walk, stop periodically to reflect on your experience of landscape and what it conjures for you. The first step is to describe the immediate landscape. Next meditate on what memories this evokes and capture them either in writing or visually. Then return to the immediate landscape and try to capture a sense of what has 'changed' during the reworking of memory. This prompt is particularly interesting to consider in contrasting places in order to evoke contrasting 'skin memories'.

Shoreline

44.0521° N, 123.0897° W

I am at the Pacific again

Outside, the sky sparks like a wet nerve.
It must be lonely to be a storm

long stems of water scattering sidelong
in a suddenly vacant wide.

Elsewhere, the coastline is a body
laying on its side

each wave slipping forward, whispering
hush

hush hush.

*

In the spring of 2012, five years before I would leave for Scotland, I make plans to move to a city in the Pacific Northwest without having ever been there. I know very little about this new environment and I wonder how different it is than the prairies and flatlands that I'm from. Photographs of Eugene, Oregon, depict lush flora and even waterfalls, but there are also evergreen forests with tree shapes that look similar to the northern treeline here. I click and zoom in on various images, scrolling past mossy wet logs along the riverside and several photographs of what appears to be the heart of the city's landscape: a bare, rocky summit called Spencer Butte.

*

I'm leaving my hometown to pursue a strange way of life that no one in my family quite understands. I've received a fellowship to study on a creative writing master's in Oregon, which means I'm suddenly able to devote two whole years to the art of writing poetry. As the daughter of immigrants from a working-class family, this opportunity gleams uneasily in front of me. It's almost unimaginable. A new path unfurls ahead, one offering the splendour of studying art and poetry, practices that I have always secretly tended to, though they appeared beyond my grasp.

It feels unreal, even unnatural, to replace my medical school prep books with poetry collections. I'd started to keep those slim volumes stacked in one corner of the bedroom I shared with my younger sister until they began to spill over into her space. For a recent poetry workshop that I took as an elective, I made collages of my poems on heavy white posterboard, then hung them on the blue wall of our bedroom with masking tape. One of the poems is called 'dusk and dove', and on the edge of the poster, I've glued a glossy magazine cut-out of a blood orange sliced cleanly in half.

I worry it's too indulgent, too whimsical, to replace the language of cell systems and human physiology with that of Linda Pastan's prosodic garden and Li-Young Lee's persimmons. It's difficult to articulate the purpose of writing poetry beyond a quest for beauty. And, to write *the perfect line* feels inconsequential to the world at large. I've not yet begun to disentangle the way art and privilege intertwine, or reflect on how my impulse to make my desires small is born from a lifetime of not seeing myself reflected in the faces of those who pursue art.

Still, while I don't yet have the language for it, poetry's importance makes itself known in a bodily way. I feel how my heart lurches when I read Nâzım Hikmet, or how my breath quickens when I turn to the work of Sylvia Plath. I'm learning how literature traces remnants of the world, remnants of the self, producing significant texts that have purpose.

*

In summer in the prairies, the clouds break open with a loud crack and we enter a period of long, unyielding thunderstorms. My life has been punctuated by these great heavy rains and their subsequent weather warnings. In the warmer months before I leave Alberta for the Pacific Northwest, sheets of rainwater – and often hail – knock against our windows, and lightning flashes in pink hues against my face. These magnificent prairie lightning storms, like the sprawling flatlands and steady foothills, are markers of this province. They are an emblem of the only home I have known up until now.

On almost any given summer day, there's a thunderstorm happening somewhere in Alberta. The formation of these storms is part of a circuit of rising and falling air. Thunderstorms are classified by *storm structures*, cycles that begin first with clouds, then updraft winds and rising air, precipitation, and finally dispersal. In my writing, I find myself characterising a place, and my closeness to it, by whether or not I see lightning there.

*

Cloud

We are at the edge of a cliff, standing on a carpet of moss mottled with jutting black rocks. I don't know how far down the drop really is because there is a gradient of hazy evening blue behind us. The sun has almost completely set and only a trickling, desperate streak of light attempts to illuminate us through the thick fog. The sky is stratified into layers. It looks like an ocean, with the most translucent blue at the very top and a haunting, deep indigo lurking in the passage below the cliff. This photograph, and the rest of them, is grainy and indistinct. They look almost like they are taken with a film camera. It is the end of 2012, and we are not using film, but an old battery-run point-and-shoot. S, one of my roommates, is moving her arms wildly to keep warm. The movement is caught on camera and gives her two blurred wings. She looks like a bird about to take off into the turbulent sky. I'm there too, next to T, another roommate, and caught in a turn toward the lens. Our bodies are imprecise outlines, with colours leaking in and out of our fuzzy forms. It looks almost like the three of us are glitching.

*

As an adult, I have very few memories of my family together, all in the same place. At Edmonton International Airport, we're gathered in one of those rare, glorious moments of togetherness. I'm close to my sisters and the three of us have tears in our eyes as we wave goodbye, because it's me this time – I'm the one who is leaving.

My father also spent much of his life chasing dreams that seemed to take him across the continent: North Edmonton, Drayton Valley, Red Deer, Camrose, and even as far away as Vancouver for a time. I'm sure there are more places I haven't listed, places he disappeared to that I don't remember because absence tends to take on the same abyssal shape in memory. Beyond this, I know that he left tracks all over Canada before I was born.

Despite the way distance compressed and expanded constantly, turning our lives away from each other, and then back again, there was always a deep love and sense of care between all five of us. That love continues to exist now, though it's sometimes translated into an anxiety we have all learned to live alongside.

I look back over my shoulder, and this becomes a repeated movement after every subsequent visit. It marks our distance from one another, and it marks me as the one who left. Of the three of us sisters, I'm the first and only one to go.

*

There are no clear boundaries between home and another home.

At the departures terminal, I prepare myself for the psychological process of moving across the Canada–US border alone for the first time. I have two large suitcases. One of them is old and made of soft red leather. It has no wheels, only a single strap that serves as a handle. The hardware is gold-plated but rusted and obscured by age. I have to lift it and let it hang by my side like an office briefcase. The other suitcase is new. It is black and cheaply made, but I bought it myself. That act, so quiet and small, completed in the anonymous way of supermarket shopping, was the first thing that made all of this feel real. I now own a piece of luggage. I'm really leaving.

Together, the suitcases tuck away the ephemera of who I am. It's strangely liberating to see the consolidation of my whole life and realise this is all I have.

*

The red leather suitcase belonged to my mother. It's worn and well-used and, though old, it holds together easily. It was this very suitcase that she brought with her on her own journey across the sky, her own passage through borderlands, first from Dar es Salaam to Toronto, and then finally to Edmonton where she eventually settled. In the 1980s, when she arrived, she was just a young girl caught at the edges of a country she didn't and couldn't know.

At the airport, I'm embarrassed by the suitcase. I think it gives away our poverty, and I place the black, synthetic, poorly built one on top of it. I want to hide a lot about myself. A guilty part of me is excited to be leaving behind the heartache and turmoil of a sometimes painful childhood. I think I don't care about Edmonton either, a place that opened up new, spindly aches within me the longer I stayed there. I'd spent my whole life trying to get away from its alpine grasp, and I didn't intend to look back.

Above all, by moving elsewhere, I want to reinvent myself, to dress myself in synthetic, mass-produced fibres; to cover my body with a body that I think is better or, at least, the same as everyone else's. These are feelings I'm only just beginning to interrogate. I want to address this identity drift more deeply but doing so requires hard work, excavating work, and even in these early years, I sense that this kind of mining will undress the wounds I've spent years hiding from my own view. At twenty-one, I don't feel like I have the tools I need to unearth myself and all the subsequent reverberations of self that I have quieted.

My mother keeps many things withheld. This is something I thought I had inherited from her until I found a voice through poetry – though poetry itself is an exercise in knowing when to withhold and when to pour. Now, I think I understand how my mother's strategy of silence is a calcification of trauma, a stronghold of gender expectations and patriarchy, and an unchosen mode of survival.

Against all of this inherited silence, I'm not good at asking the right questions, and it isn't until I move away that I start really listening. I try not to linger on all that has been lost in the widening chasm of time between one uncommunicative generation and the next. Part of me thinks I can fill in the gaps with crafted language.

I'm not yet experienced enough with my chosen artform to realise that lyricism ends up creating more objects than it uncovers truths.

When I ask about that day, the day she left one home for another dream, she tells me that she arrived at the airport in Canada for the first time with her red suitcase and wearing a sundress and summer shoes. My mother laughs when she tells this story because after more than thirty years of living in this cold winter country, she understands the absurdity of such an image.

Imagine what everyone thought. Who is this foolish girl wearing a summer dress in the middle of winter?

*

Updraft

The caption is *hot springs and glowsticks*. I didn't take this picture but I wish I did, because it is that rare kind of landscape photo that captures the essence of place without trying. Fog creates spectral layers, four of them semi-distinct. But these layers are likely made up of a multitude of layers themselves, indistinguishable at this camera quality. After walking a quarter of a mile from the car park, we arrive at the dark hues of a primeval woodland. It is made even darker by a looming ground cloud. This photo must be taken from the same cliff, but

> looking outward, straight ahead. It captures the ecosystem's verticality. A dark mound is visible in the centre, and other hills roll in and out of clarity behind it. Conifer trees, perhaps Douglas firs, cluster at their tops and overrun their edges. I'm not sure anymore, but it might be Rider Creek in the distance, taking on a holographic, bright blue hue.

*

Before I ever visit Dar es Salaam, the place where my parents grew up, I find myself imagining what the city might look and feel like. I tend to imagine these sensations mostly on my skin. I'm obsessed with skin, my own skin especially, as a barrier and a kind of borderland of its own. Skin is porous enough to let heat, humidity and sea spray diffuse through.

As well as a settler, I'm a second-generation immigrant. I've read that this generation is sometimes called the *hinge* generation. This term makes me think of a doorway, a threshold of some kind, with a version of me swinging through it. *Hinge* is a beautifully ambiguous word. Sometimes I feel a great responsibility, thinking of myself as the connective tissue between my parents' lived experience and the possible knowledge of generations after me. Other times, the word feels like permission to let go, to swing in any direction I please across time and space and generational murkiness.

Over the years, I've grown interested in how this unique position, this hinging position, has guided how I interpret, access and even reproduce my parents' displacement from their ancestral homelands. I embody a profound plurality, one that has simultaneously involved both turning away from my heritage and looking at it straight on.

*

Though his ancestry goes back to India, my father was born in Mtwara, a Tanzanian village built around a deep-water port and surrounded by a jungle saturated with butterfly trees. Its proximity to the Equator and the Indian Ocean results in a tropical wet and dry climate. Beyond that, he lived in the coastal city of Dar es Salaam. When he tells me about Tanzania, these scenes are tinged with the vibrant characteristics of places I can barely imagine, and the ocean takes on a mythological quality most of all.

My own childhood features thunderstorms and heavy snowfall in a landlocked region of the Midwest. One of my clearest memories is of lingering outside late at night when I'm eight years old. My father is next to me, tinkering with our old, second-hand family van, its sheen of gold dissipating into the night's winter darkness. I remember the mechanical slide of its back door sweeping shut. I remember looking up into the sky and seeing the chilling, poignant glow of the Northern Lights, a mesmerising spectacle right there, right above our ordinary street, right above our ordinary townhouse and front yard.

In one of my father's favourite childhood memories, he rises very early in the morning on a typically hot and humid day. A new Bollywood film is playing in the only cinema nearby. My father adores the cinema. He's desperate to see the film. It's a day-long bike ride from Mtwara to the nearest town, and although everyone calls it an impossible task, he takes the journey on the wet red-clay roads that cut across the coastal jungle. This memory has a different texture than mine. It's rife with heat and moisture and blurry, quick movement. Yet, underscoring both these recollections is the same feeling of adventure, the crystallised knowledge that we are witnessing something special, something beautiful that is poised toward meaning.

When he reminisces about Tanzania, my father's voice grows warm and wistful. I hold these moments close. I have gleaned that when he arrived in Canada by way of forced migration, he struggled to find financial stability as a racialised first-generation immigrant. His recollections of East Africa are tinged with the generosity of retrospection, a sepia-toned nostalgia that erases hardship. He was only a teenager when he left, and he has since amassed decades of longing for football games, the local cinema, the kebab shop, his childhood friends, bike rides between villages, and perhaps most of all, his mother – my daddima.

When I leave for Oregon, I make a choice that glistens with multiple modes of opportunity and privilege. Now I think of how difficult it must have been for my father to be displaced outside of his control, to be young and dislocated, with a long history of young and dislocated ancestors behind him. To carry within him a fragment of history left in the destructive wake of British colonialism.

*

Rising

> It is pitch-black outside. I can't tell you what exists in the background, whether there are trees, rivers, cliffs or hills. One object bleeds into another in darkness, one black stone becomes another black stone at night. The three of us are in the middle of the photograph, lit up vaguely by the camera's flash. This is how I know it is raining. Raindrops fall in front of the lens, and they are captured as long streaks that slice the photo into thirds. S tries to catch the raindrops in her mouth while holding a neon-green glowstick in one hand and her blue and white towel in the other. Meanwhile, T looks into the sky ambivalently. I'm next to both of them, chin tilted high into the air, eyes closed and arms

held out at my sides as if I would willingly let the storm devour me. We are bundled up in our waterproof clothes, doubly wet from our swim and from the notorious, ongoing Oregonian rainfall.

*

I begin to build a life in Eugene, acclimatising to the humid climate. In the spring and summer, I develop hay fever and I'm advised by one of my roommates that eating the local wild honey will help. At a little alcove of shops across from Amazon Park, the opulent green space I live near and walk through hundreds of times, I find what I'm looking for: Capella Market, a haven of local and organic foods sold in bulk.

I enter the market carrying a glass jam jar that I fill up with pure gold syrupy antidote and, when I return home, I eat it by the spoonful. I hope that this expensive raw clover honey will trick the Pacific Northwest into accepting that I belong here, into convincing it that I'm not an invasive species, that I'm not a stranger to this environment and its abundance of grass pollen. Even if, in reality, it's the pollen that is foreign to *my* body.

I have a propensity for rainfall and stormy weather, and I find myself excited for the wet and moody atmosphere of Oregon in the winter. But the cooler months don't provide much by way of relief. While northern Alberta is cold, with temperatures that sometimes dip to minus 40°C, it's an unexpectedly sunny area of the world. Eugene is wet and moody and *dark*. I develop seasonal affective disorder, and it pairs listlessly with homesickness. I order a happy lamp. I ask myself why I ever moved away. I miss my family. I miss T, the boyfriend I left behind in Edmonton after three gorgeous months of youthful dating.

In the darkness of my friend J's apartment, with his signature Bolognese simmering on the stovetop, I write poems about all the things I miss. We read extracts to each other. We are creative and rife with artistic potential. Tanzania starts to edge into my work, and I translate my father's stories into imagery and lineation. I capture what I think is the right shade of green for pigeon pea trees and I try to render the shape of a sisal tree's basal rosettes onto the page. These poems are bucolic and rooted in landscape; they are imaginative and not quite true. But I think something important is happening. I think I'm finding a lost part of myself – or I'm learning to love those parts of myself that I'd tried to wring away. I'm even beginning to write about my childhood in Canada, a place that I realise I could not write about, could not feel tenderness toward, until I left.

I bring these poems to workshop. In that first year of my master's, I'm the only person of colour enrolled in the poetry strand across three years. It's 2012, and poetry like mine is seen as marginal, inaccessible, sentimental and *exotic* by the larger industry. I love many of my peers and my teachers, but I feel like an outlier in this classroom. I'm in the footnotes of what is claimed as the universal experience.

Eventually, another student corners me at the local pub after class. We are seated at the back patio and lit by streaks of lamplight. Cheap beer and popcorn kernels litter the ground. I don't drink and he is very drunk. He compliments my poetry. He says he thinks I'm going to be 'really good'. He's several years older and appears to have some literary experience. So, when he leans in and imparts his words of wisdom, I believe them. But this single sentence is a seed that lodges deep within me, that undoes months of work.

But you write too many poems about being Indian.

*

I'm often told that I write too much about the body. A past version of myself – the girl grappling with how to know herself against the rocky silhouette of Spencer Butte – revised the body away. This is painful because of what was lost in the process, but also because of all the accompanying shame. Sometimes, I feel so much shame across so many intersections. It's unbearable and makes me want to retreat. What are the implications of telling a queer woman of colour that she writes too much about the body? What is the narrative framework, the assumption, that builds around me with every new thing I make and tentatively let exist out of my control?

*

In every family home we moved to, no matter how tiny or cramped, there have always been two photographs displayed prominently in the living room. These black and white stills depict my grandparents.

Everyone tells me I look like my daddima, and yes, I see it. I see the way I reflect history when I clip my hair back, pushing aside my fringe and staring directly into the mirror with a concentrated gaze. I have her round face and we share moles across our foreheads. The shape of her body beneath her sari unfolds into a soft figure, and I tend to replicate her stance in my own photographs.

When my father's illness worsens, he begins to frequently dream of his mother by his bedside. He says her ghost is in the room with him all night, and he tells her stories about Canada, the life he has made here in this country of unfathomable snow-white cold. In a different dream, he tells me they walk together barefoot across the overgrown grass behind his childhood home in the jungles of Nanyamba.

In *Going Toward the Ghost*, academic and poet Jane Wong considers how 'social, historical, and political contexts "haunt" the work of contemporary Asian American poets'. Her examinations of 'a poetics of haunting' and of what narratives lurk under our present lived experiences make me think of how our histories and traumas are passed down through generations. I sense this haunting, I sense these ghosts, in the stories my father tells me. These dreams feel potent with a kind of intangible truth. I start to feel the ghosts rise like smoke in my own body and, of course, they appear in my own written work.

My daddima passed away when my father was young. Born and raised in Tanzania, she never left her country for another country, and at twenty-one years old, I have not yet made plans to visit her grave.

*

Precipitation

> The rain is harder and quicker now. Three figures are visible, but just barely, and they are closer to the camera this time. On the left edge of the photograph is a gritty, teal-coloured stripe. It creates an accidental and slightly holographic effect, though it looks strangely like it belongs there. I am not in this photograph, so I think I must have taken it.

*

My mother says she was a village girl, a small-town girl.

After I move to Oregon, I begin to have this recurring dream. It's of my mother as a young girl living in Tanzania. Her hair, wild and long, its texture much curlier than my own, is plaited loosely behind her back. She is running fast in the deep, viscous heat. In the dream, I am an observer, and her figure is a discontinuous blur against a thick line of trees I don't quite recognise. When she finally comes to a stop, instead of my mother, I see a slender adult gazelle in her place.

Years later, after this dream has melted away from my subconscious, my mother sends me a photograph of herself as a child. It's a family portrait taken in Dar es Salaam with eight different people in the frame. This includes all of her siblings and her mother and father. It must have been taken at a celebration of some kind because they are posed behind an elaborate meal, complete with stacks of roti and at least twenty glass bottles of cola. Not long after the photograph is taken, in a story that isn't mine to tell, my mother leaves her family home to live in the village she alludes to. I download the photograph and zoom in to examine all eight faces that, in some small way, must resemble my own.

My mother says this is the only photograph she has of all of them, her whole family, caught in a rare, glorious moment of togetherness. She calls it her *one memory*.

*

My friend R once remarked on the importance of storms in my poetry. There is something simultaneously special and strange about being seen through one's work. It's true that I have always liked the storms I've grown up with. I have childhood memories of seeing dark clouds in the sky gather, and of sensing the quality of the air change. I loved accumulating that *outdoor smell* on my skin, especially when the sky was dense and ethereal, and my arms turned to goose flesh as the temperature began to turn.

Between the ages of five and ten, I fought constantly to be outside regardless of the weather, forcing my parents to chase me around the neighbourhood, and once, up the tall deciduous tree in the front yard of our old townhouse. Even back then, I always seemed to be straying away, trying my best to slip out of their grasp and into independence.

When warm winds from the Pacific Ocean meet with the Rocky Mountains, they sometimes cause what is called an 'Albertan clipper', a fast-moving, low-pressure storm track. These winds travel over the mountains and eventually develop into the storms we reckon with in the prairies. It is turbulent at the meeting point of contrast, when something elemental travels so far out of its way to an elsewhere place, when the wind remains in continuous movement between ocean coastline and interior plains.

Though I convince myself I am drawn to thunderstorms because they remind me of the innocence of girlhood, of feeling freedom outdoors, I think there's also this—

I must have always loved storms for their poetry.

*

Dispersal

And then all of us are caught dancing in the storm. What was merely imprecise before becomes a total loss of shape. I disintegrate almost completely into the tempestuous background. Lightning or no lightning, I love the Pacific Northwest as I have come to know it

almost ocean/
almost earth/
almost sky.

55.9533° N, 3.1883° W

Echoes in the garden

Stones of Scotland / '(a)version'

Faith, like everything, has a form. I wake up some mornings, and prayer finds me as naturally as language. The ritual of recitation tugs me forward into the whole of my day with its vast energy. Last night, I dreamed that my younger sister and I were together and preparing for evening dua – though we are, in actuality, over fourteen thousand kilometres apart and with a deep, mysterious ocean between us.

This dream is strange. Of all of us in my immediate family, my younger sister and I have strayed the furthest from our faith. But it also reminds me that, *yes*, I carry a strong remnant of spirituality within me. I catch myself praying all the time, unthinkingly, as if it is a bodily process as automatic as breathing. Prayer even appears within the metaphysical boundaries of my dreams. I teeter back and forth in its wind, participating in push and pull: I practise my faith and then I let it go. I pray to Allah and then I displace Them to the back of my mind. I am aligned and then I am not.

/

I have a complicated relationship with my Muslim upbringing. When I think I need it the most, its comfort and belief, my faith eludes me.

In the spring of 2020, two things coalesced. This season marked the first lockdown in Scotland, and it marked the holy month of Ramadan. In self-isolation, afraid and lonely, I found myself withdrawing. I was unable to feel connected to most things, but I felt especially disconnected from Islam. I was displaced from my family, who remain the strongest link I have to my faith. And during this season, the distance between Edmonton and Edinburgh seemed greater than ever, too great a distance for even my dreams to travel.

As a result, Ramadan took on a different, unrecognisable shape, one edged with trepidation. I responded by resolutely listening to prayers through my old phone speakers, though they were ribbed with static. I tried to appreciate digital moments with my family more completely. My mother and father and aunts and uncles all separately sent me images of spring flowers annotated with blessings in lieu of videos of family gatherings. And in my pursuit to feel close to my faith despite these new chasms, I vowed to be more self-reflective, meditative, and generous with myself and with others. At a time when relationships felt out of reach, I wanted to connect more deeply with my local surroundings – and ultimately, as became evident over those asymmetrical months, with the natural world.

Although I wouldn't realise it until much later, over those first months of lockdown, I was *collecting*. I was beginning to squirrel away the anxiety of the pandemic in my body, which has unfurled now into its new, marked and unequivocal margins. I didn't know it then, but four years into the future, I would be weighed down by these abrasions. Eventually, my body would transform into the kind of emotional and physical shape that could just barely contain the disquiet.

As the cracked screen of my phone became not quite a home but a place I certainly lived in, someone I trust advised me to find a way to *dislodge what is lodged* – swim in a river, perhaps, she said.

I thought a lot about those words, how they made me notice something invasive and unbelonging in my body. Within a few months, I was also forced to turn to the question of how to contend with the inevitable act of *lodging*. The process. The way by which trauma leaks into a system, a body, and calcifies.

/

Earlier that month, I was meant to read at my friend Pratyusha's launch for her work *bulbul calling* in a forest near London. This was one of many things made impossible by the pandemic. Instead, her hand-sewn pamphlet arrived in the mail near the start of Ramadan. Both this fact and the book's significance to me as an object became important to my spring observation: I began an intentional practice of reading a poem by a South Asian woman outdoors every day, and I started with the pages of *bulbul calling*. I thought doing so might help me feel the connections I longed for, and even, perhaps, help me to dislodge. The poem as it was reified against the contours of spring – that was my river.

With mosques closed for the foreseeable future and communities scattered across the city, this routine and its rhythm were, I believed, one way I could feel closer to other voices and ultimately, through intentionality, to my religion. It became an act of religious observation and a form of spirituality in itself. I began my endeavour at the start of Ramadan and continued until Eid. In this way, walking and prayer intertwined.

/

Seeds and their scattering are irrefutably linked with metaphors of displacement: of errantry, of wandering, of migration. Agents of pollination are part of this cycle: the orchid, the moth, the wind. This is a compelling mythology.

In *Cultivation and Catastrophe: The Lyric Ecology of Modern Black Literature*, the scholar Sonya Posmentier writes that 'hybridity and diaspora are etymologically related to organic life' and she suggests this signals the need to consider these cultural concepts as 'living metaphors'. As I walked through Edinburgh's various landscapes, I couldn't help but reflect on movement and migration. Amongst those green spaces, I found my thoughts automatically straying to reflect on my diasporic identity.

I had decided early on that one of my treks during Ramadan would be toward Salisbury Crags, Edinburgh's city cliffside; I was drawn to their unavoidable proof of this city's natural verticality. One morning that spring, I had set out with the intention of walking there, but weather cut short my journey. I found myself scattered instead near Easter Road, where I was jostled by the wind and unable to continue to the path that would eventually lead me to the foot of the crags. Instead, moving against a rough ecological friction, I turned abruptly and made my way to Regent Road, succumbing to the vectors of strong winds that gasped around me.

The wind speed that day was thirty-one miles per hour. According to the Beaufort Scale, I could call this a *moderate gale*. The moderate gale ushered me away from what I knew and toward the unexpected, as if I was a seed being carried along to some resting place where I'd eventually root, and bloom, and flourish.

'Wind was the invisible force powering colonial expansion,' writes poet and interdisciplinary artist J.R. Carpenter. The Beaufort Scale informs the structure of her multimodal piece *This is a Picture of Wind*, where poetry is 'randomly generated in part by live wind data and in part by the inexorable passage of time'. I felt taut within these ideas, within the inability to make my own path here in Edinburgh. I thought about the strong pull of imperceptible forces that led me to myself over a long history of forced displacement.

The wind, I have come to realise, is a cartographer – a mixture of biology, art and technology. It is a system that surveys the past and tells the future.

/

I'm both uncertain and reassured when it comes to definitions of diaspora. I find the image of the wayward seed compelling, but I'm also distraught by it. I crave rootedness but then I'm jolted by the sharp reminder of what I ache to root into – a place where modernity and Westernisation, heteropatriarchy and capitalism are prioritised.

Writer and documentarian Dionne Brand writes, 'belonging does not interest me. I had once thought that it did. Until I examined the underpinnings. One is mislead when one looks at the sails and majesty of tall ships instead of their cargo.' When I *do* lament for a homeland to which I belong, which happens regularly in spite of myself, I understand I am doing so as a reaction. I employ the diction of difference in response to the violent misrecognitions of my identity by the nation I live in. A tried and tested way for a country to uphold its physical and metaphorical borders, to sew shut with finality its own identity, is to create a borderland in which someone is always feeling unmoored, and unaccepted, and *un-homed*.

In *Insurgent Empire*, Priyamvada Gopal interrogates 'the tenacious assumption that the most significant conceptions of "freedom" are fundamentally "Western" in provenance'. As I reflect on belonging, I think also of the mathematical asymptote: the long line that can get close, so close, to touching its nearby curve. Line and curve are in proximity, the difference between them almost becoming zero. But they do not touch, and they never will. The asymptote is the limit. I am the limit by which the oppressor can know themselves.

All of this because once my ancestors were forced by the wind and arrived elsewhere.

/

As an immigrant and settler in Canada, I, too, am marked by Westernised modernity. I am part of an ongoing colonial precedent. Although I am easily marked by differences that place me at the very fringes of commonality within certain nation states – by aspects like my race and my religion – my personal archive is also filled with the lived experience of being educated in the West, of working in the West, and of submitting to academic models of the West, where the concept of decolonising the institution is contradicted by the institution's very existence on stolen land.

Drifting, scattering, planting, rooting, blossoming, drinking in the Scottish rains, being pulled by its wind – *yes*, I embody all of this. And simultaneously, all of this is rupturing. I double or triple or multiply into an octet, continuously, until I am relational to everything all at once: river and stone and wind. Until I am the asymptote journeying forever toward infinity.

/

In the UK, three years after my green project, pandemic restrictions ease and I find myself reading my work aloud to predominantly white audiences. Under harsh lighting, with my body pointed toward a room of unfamiliar faces, I recite my poetry about the solitary heron at Lochend Park, about elk and their muscular strength in Jasper, about Florence, Oregon, where oysters gather on oceanic ridges of the Pacific Coast. These poems are tinged with the complexity of my Muslim faith. I river between sexual desire, queerness and womanhood, touching on the way these aspects weave together with my religion. The elk, their antlers poised against green vine, are symbolic of a lesson: *it is as if Allah himself has approached me* to impart Their divine knowledge. I want to undercut insidious thought processes that categorise me as: either a Muslim writer or a nature writer, but never both.

Kazim Ali writes, 'the body is not the opposite of the spirit, nor are physical matters oppositional to abstract ideas of the spirit'. I have grappled with my sense of self in a world that thrives on dichotomy. I have felt the grief of trying to split myself apart, as if body and spirit, as if faith and queer desire, are incongruent. As if I have to close off one to wholly belong in the other.

I return to Ali's work often; it was his poetry that first made me feel safe within my identity as a queer Muslim woman. Through my writing, through its sinews of imagery and introspection, I attempt to accept the alternating calcifications and softnesses of my body. I try to find a way to accept my body as it exists beside my religion. Eventually, over time, I allow myself to feel at peace when I pray and when I don't. I allow myself to feel distraught when prayer eludes me. I allow my body to be my body, whether engaged in the religious experience of counting or gathered in the arms of an intimate partner. I remind myself that belief is also a plot of land on which we can grow the seeds of what we love.

/

The Stones of Scotland is a monument at Regent Road Park that includes thirty-two stones arranged in a circle, and in the centre of that circle is a pine tree. On the day that I am displaced by the wind, I stood instead within that orbital boundary and looked straight ahead. From there, I had a clear view of the glaciated remains that marked the crags which had been my original destination.

The stones had travelled from Aberdeen, Stirling, East Ayrshire and other areas of Scotland, all to be eventually displaced here in Edinburgh. Grey granite, red sandstone, andesite – all of them sit side by side. Lichen and moss hold them in place. They are part of a geological and geometrical organisation. I am aware of their past lives, but will only ever know them here, where their context is changed by the crags behind them, the tree between them, the city around them. By my very presence that day, accidental as it was.

Seeing them there together, I find myself reflecting on the distances between arriving and becoming. I think, *when does a collection of stones begin to house the moss of a different place?*

That day, I make a spiritual space for new stones and the stones I carry, always: the mossy rock from Alberta, the wet, mooring agate of the Oregon coast, the red clay from Mtwara. I think of how, even in my imagination, these areas have changed over time, echoing with new movements. It would be three years, for example, before I would see Alberta's shield of rocks again. They would become more and more blurred and unreal in memory.

Here, at the Stones of Scotland, adrift next to the Scots pine, I read Pratyusha's poem, '(a)version', which feels serendipitous. After all, this reading is a version of what I set out to accomplish, a different version than I expected. Its own peculiar kind of aversion. Its words echo on the periphery of this multidirectional journey, where I became scattered only to find myself next to a scattering of stones.

Wind is that sensation, that deep push and pull, that grazes my face, my neck, my arms, *my skin*. Though created at the meeting of contradiction – high and low pressure – there is something in-between about it too, as if wind itself is the swinging hinge. In Pratyusha's poem, rife with the Ganga River, there is the suggestion of what we carry, or even *how* we carry across multiplicity: 'my grandmother gives me a shell, because I should keep the water with me.'

/

I wake up one morning that spring and feel compelled to recite tasbih: Subhan Allah, at least thirty-three times. My body relaxes and my anxiety quietens. If invasive experiences and feelings have lodged into my body, at least there is also *this*. The way the body might remember something ancestral, the way memories thread from generation to generation. The way love slips in, unnoticed.

Lochend Park / 'ghazals'

I step outside into the rain. Today, the sky is dark and the gorse curls into itself, its yellows murky. We are allowed a few minutes outdoors every day, and every day, I lace up my boots in the afternoon. My body takes note of how the weather changes. Rain and then high winds. I tuck away my copy of *bulbul calling* in my rucksack, making sure to wrap it up in something waterproof. I'm worried about the water distorting its lilac cover and ruining the delicate stitching down its spine. It's a beautiful handmade book and, at this point in lockdown, it represents a way to feel tactilely connected to people I love, to touch and preserve an object that reaches materially across an otherwise lonely space.

/

On the first day of Ramadan, I make my way to Lochend Park, and its body of water, close to where I live in Edinburgh. As I walk, my thoughts begin to flicker into the past, to the Bow River in Calgary, Alberta. Briefly, even if only in my imagination, I'm transported back to Calgary where I stop at the river to look over its unruly edge. In this imagined scene, my reflection quivers, cut through by rocks and the movement of wild waters. Every time I visit, I'm always surprised by the strength of the current and the river's vastness.

In 2013, southern and central Alberta experienced heavy rainfall, some of the worst in the province's history. The relentless rain triggered catastrophic flooding. The Bow River tested its seams and thousands of people were displaced. Before that, before anyone understood how close to disaster we were, I booked a three-hour Greyhound bus trip from Edmonton to Calgary, so I could visit my long-distance boyfriend. It turned out to be the last bus travelling into the city until after the flood. I remember it was rerouted from its final stop in downtown, near where the Bow River intersects the city, to a strip mall in the northwest.

At Lochend Park, I look up at the sky and feel sensations of wind and water mix on my face. I'm jostled by the memory of the Bow River and struck by how weather can pull me back through time. I think of Sara Ahmed, who writes that 'the Narrator remembers with and through her body', as the rain seeps into my skin. What is the distance between departure and arrival when the journey is a metaphysical one? Between arrival and becoming? When is a loch no longer a loch but an extension of my imagination.

Emerging from my memory of Calgary, I think it's possible I'm always in a liquid state of matter, never quite arriving, never quite solid in form.

/

It's raining the kind of rain that's felt asymmetrically. The sky is clutching at the tail end of every drop, still convincing itself to let go. My body feels the same way, unwilling to let go, unwilling to release all my pent-up grief, while simultaneously unable to stopgap its leaking. Like sweat, grief pools on my skin as if slithering out from within me. I blot it away. I find myself under a sycamore tree, covered by its five-lobed leaves and sheltered by a hundred small dark green hands.

The sycamore is a sieve and rain sifts through lightly. Water petals onto my mouth, my eyelids, my neck. I think of that moment years ago when I stepped off the Greyhound disoriented, heels sinking into a trench of water in a flooded parking lot. It's both eerie and exquisite how the feeling of rain can evoke the familiarity of all other rains while it defamiliarises a place at the same time. When it flooded, the Bow River flowed through Calgary at three times its peak levels. I had never seen the city submerged in so much water. I think of Alberta as a dry place.

/

I read 'ghazals', the first poem in *bulbul calling* at Lochend Park with the water birds. I can't help but think that they so easily tendril longing, winding back and forth, a nostalgic tracing on the water. Like the loch itself, they are perfectly poised to become symbols.

[he is here]
[his voice is here]
[the soft stir at night]

I think I hear the voice that this poem elegises the same way I feel the rain: askance. The same way I see the birds: flickering through the near-bare trees. The same way words flicker through the permeable but still contained square brackets in Pratyusha's poetry.

/

The ghazal is a musical poetic form. It's written in couplets and, traditionally, it was sung aloud. It's originally an Arabic verse form, but it also has roots in Iran, India and Pakistan. The ghazal ends on a lyric note, a note that poet Bhanu Kapil says *should be torn from the body like a sob.*

The word 'ghazal' reminds me of the word 'ginan', which comes from the Sanskrit word 'jnan', and means religious, contemplative or reflective knowledge. It can also mean song or recitation. I think I want to hold the two together, ghazal and ginan, the love poem and the devotional song. Like ghazals, ginans were traditionally shared largely through oral tradition. Each one is composed in a particular raga, and different ginans have different purposes; some are recited at evening prayer, others at specific religious ceremonies. For hundreds of years, my ancestors have been reciting ginan as part of their religious devotions. History is tethered to this tradition, as is the preservation of local languages. Ginans and their rhythms mark my inherited memory like a metronome.

I have written ghazals to varying degrees of success. One of these attempts is a prayer poem, where traditions of both forms interweave. Agha Shahid Ali said the ghazal is defined by *constant longing*. I think of my father singing ginan at Jama'at twenty years ago and almost fourteen thousand kilometres away. One reminds me of the other, and longing cracks open my makeshift shelter under the sycamore tree.

/

At the end of 'ghazals', in its final verse, there are GPS coordinates. These coordinates mark the place of loss, a place that doubly represents endurance and exhale and slipping away—

[12°24'27.8"N76°43'18.1"E]
[his breath is here]

The rain and this poem have fused into a reminder. Amidst a grey sky that withholds and reveals its moisture in parts, I am transported into a memory of my daddima's burial site.

In January 2019, on my very first and only visit to Tanzania, my father and I drove forty-five minutes outside of Dar es Salaam to the Kabristan where my grandmother was buried. My father hadn't seen his mother's gravesite since he was a teenager. This truth was one of the remnants of his displacement. On the drive over, I had been distracted by the trees outside the car window, their clusters of tropical branches adorned with giant leaves. I thought of the way they contrasted with the needled pine and spruce I grew up with, evergreens that lined highway roads and turned them into forest corridors. I wanted to be able to name them all, as if to fully realise them, and tried to take note of any unique traits: the colour of bark, the shape and size of flowers. As we neared the graveyard, my father pointed out that most of them were mango trees.

The day was too hot for the two of us who had acclimatised to Canada's northern temperatures. As the heat pressed down on us, we walked along the Kabristan's rows upon rows. We spent a long time searching for her grave, peering at faded names before moving on. The graveyard keepers helped us, offering watering cans to bless the new houses of other familiar names with streaming water. To bless the soil with water. Beside us there was a river. It roiled, churning with its own strength.

Eventually, we learned that several gravesites had flooded and fallen into that river. They'd washed away during an unusually heavy rainstorm only a few years ago. It was likely that my grandmother's grave was one of them. While in Tanzania, Kutchi, my first lost language, was coming back to me slowly. It was growing around my grotesquely Western body, reminding me of my ever-present penumbra, the edges of a history that both does and doesn't belong to me. I remember I understood him. I can almost even remember exactly how he said it, the graveyard keeper, when he told my father that my grandmother's grave fell into the river.

I can't speak the words now. I only recall the sensation of heat and the flood of the river. And I remember my father's grief, which always has a certain clarity to it. We spent all afternoon looking for her plot of land. It was once there, and then it was gone.

/

In 'ghazals', I am drawn to the precision of the coordinates. Each number is an assertion. It casts off ephemerality. Each number tells you exactly where to find the ghosts. What is the distance between my father's memory and the woman I never met, not even there, in the quadrants of her final resting place? What is the distance between the mango tree of one of my ancestral homelands and the small spruce tree I planted in my childhood home? These are the kinds of distances and intimacies I hold in my body. These measurements are the sensations of rustling. Of blood and of sweaty skin.

The Kabristan is always changing, new bodies, new memories receding into damp dirt and becoming a part of the earth. Water pours over all of it, whether from the thin neck of a watering can, or whether from the weeping sky.

/

My father keeps a square of fabric in his wallet. It's patterned and small, frayed at the edges. He slips it behind the photograph of me and my sisters he also keeps forever tucked away. I learn that it has always been there. It's a strip of fabric from one of my grandmother's old dresses, yellow and white.

I think of the thresholds in Pratyusha's poem: in its voice, its permanence, its precision, its music, its flood. And I can also hear her voice in it. My daddima's. A new and imagined sound in a re-remembered language. It rises from the roots of the surrounding trees, from the drifting water birds, from my own reflection in a river several years ago.

When we learned about the flood and how it had washed away the last ties her physical body had to this graveyard, my father stood for a while at the place it might have been. After a few minutes, he sat down on a nearby rock and asked me to film him. From his wallet, he took out the square of fabric, setting it gently on his lap. Then he sang. The sound of his prayer tore from his body like a sob.

Calton Hill / 'mirage'

I spend time identifying the trees. I do this as best as I can because I still struggle with the nomenclature. Their names – *oak, beech, lime, willow* – ebb away from my tongue like fine mist. Close and then far, tangible and then somehow formless. These words are mysteries. The trees are a language that I can feel but can't speak.

Why do the names of trees escape me? My inability to retain this information reminds me of how, growing up, it was difficult for me to memorise and recite the Quran in Arabic. There are some knowledges that I can't quite grasp, that slip away the more steadfastly I try to secure myself to them. It's almost as if the more I want to identify with these ways of witnessing the world, the more evanescent they are.

/

My earliest memory of prayer is also an early memory of learning how to read. I'm six years old and in my parents' bedroom. We moved from this townhouse shortly after, but somehow, more than other places I've lived, this particular home and its small blueprint is stark and defined in my memory. It's the first home I can remember; a unit at the end of a line of adjoined buildings, four families sharing walls against the backdrop of flat Albertan prairies somewhere beyond and unseen.

I imagine arriving at the nightstand at my father's bedside. This is where he keeps his copy of his Quran, with its dark green cover. Beautifully bound, it is a bilingual edition with Arabic in the first half. I scan the script, black ink swooping across its pages in cursive peaks and percussions. It dips and travels and swells like the unending note of a long breeze. I've memorised a few words but not enough to decode the language that I will never learn. The Quran is only meant to be recited in Arabic. I gaze at the two slippery hearts, Arabic and its English translation, and something in me stirs. I want to know what these pages hold. I think they will help me better understand my father. I switch to the English side.

While in primary school, I had been focused on learning how to read. How to shape English letters into their precise markings – tall, tree-like letters next to small eddies. There is an emphasis on *this* language, and this language is a storm. With its ongoing rains, English overruns the few hours every Saturday morning that I spent practising my duas.

On those Saturdays, I lag behind in my recitation. But, with an uneasy pride, I find I can quickly memorise a verse in English. My prayer slips away from me, imperceptibly.

/

The walk up Calton Hill is a leisurely one. There is, of course, the darkness that runs like a current underneath my moving feet. Every day, there is a news report, a headline, and the creeping worry and sensation of danger. The lockdown extends ahead of us, slick and unknowable, longer every day. In a strange and curious way, it is the reason I am here right now, being deliberate, intentional and slow in my climb. In confronting fear and loss, I find I want to be more mindful of what I have in the present moment.

The pine scores through these thoughts. Pine, at least, I know. So much of it lingers in Edmonton. I remember how pine rested at the fringes of long working days in laborious jobs with unpredictable hourly schedules. I remember my mother tumbling through the door after a ten-hour shift. All those inviting trees and others like it crawled across the landscape that was only ever on the periphery of our thoughts rather than at the centre of our experiences. They were green accents to indoor lives dedicated to survival.

/

As I continue climbing the steep path up Calton Hill, I breathe hard into the cool spring air. I think of how surprising all of that is to me now. As an adult, porous to creativity and privileged with the time and the resources to create art, my relationship to nature emerges in my poetry again and again like a talisman. Riven with memories of love in the foothills, scrambling the heights of Mount Yamnuska, or hiking in the forests around Barrier Lake, these landscapes hold great and sincere importance in my heart.

When I think back on my childhood, to what was passed down to me from my family, certain memories are at the forefront. My days moved forward according to prayer: reciting evening dua, flicking beads on a tasbih, getting dressed for Jama'at Khana. And by other ways of gathering – not gathering the names of trees, but *gatherings* centred around the names of recipe ingredients and long hours of cooking. Familial gatherings at the table that prompted laughter and storytelling. All of these memories in persistent city settings, triangulated between our house, our mosque and our places of work.

Even now, when I visit my childhood home, this is how we spend our time together, how our love manifests. Time – as reflected in the way I notice and attend to the world – moves differently.

/

I take a break and look out for those specific traits that match the species in a photo I've taken identifying the local flora. Doing so allows me to take a break every so often without being obvious about it. This reveals to me that, despite my performance of self-acceptance, I still house shame toward my body and mistakenly see its needs as flaws. During one of these stops is when I notice my favourite type of tree recorded in the corner of the image. Birch. I think of how the silver birch in Alberta and Edinburgh are not exactly the same. For a moment, I miss those rickety arms that glowed white in the dark prairie evenings, rows and rows of trees stretched out on the highway just outside of the city. How long has it been since I've seen birch like that, nestled densely alongside those northern journeys?

And just like the birch trees, my own body in Alberta and Edinburgh is not exactly the same. I'm so rarely at the outskirts of a city now, slinging through quiet country roads. It's been well over a year since I've driven anywhere, least of all on the highways outside my hometown, all those regions where I used to focus my gaze so intensely on the flat, long, provincial road. When the birch trees resided only on the edges.

/

The silver birch shifts shape and my edges blur too. I know how a landscape alters a body, alters the 'I', alters the subject and her imagination. Here, at Calton Hill, I face the direction of the sea. I see the stratified layers of city and water. Elsewhere, my neck may turn upward to follow a mountain, rife with blossoming flowers and carved with the paths of large animals. Elsewhere still, the reeds of a jungle growing out from red clay.

Walking up the hill, beside hazel and ash – or so I think – I leave footprints alongside the footprints of strangers, beside everyone and everything here, unseen across time. The squirrels and beetles and trail runners. We share this experience and find commonality, crossing the borders of linear time by way of root and seed and dirt. For some, it is a chemical understanding. Language, the draw of one species toward another, is a simple case of instinct.

For the duration of this one step, when I lift my leg, my muscle memory sends me back in time. It's as if I'm back on a path in Kananaskis again, the dirt of multiple places commingling under the rubber soles of my hiking boots.

And I remember too, that a body – bodies – also alter a landscape: through consumption, impression and silence. It's here, with the unfolding cityscape and seascape in the distance, that I open the lilac cover of *bubul calling*. Today's poem is 'mirage', a piece filled with pungencies and heat: 'echoes are drying up [land is drying up]'.

/

In his work on time, Blackness and landscape, poet Jason Allen-Paisant writes, 'the possibilities of landscape are underpinned by socio-economic dynamics rooted in a colonial history and its afterlives'. I think of my desperation to know the names of trees, and how this anxiety sometimes eclipses the real-life experience of being amongst them. Acknowledging this makes me uneasy – how I allow a Western naming convention inherited by the history of empire to tower over my bodily memories and stories and experiences. All my life, I have reckoned with the perception that some information is deemed more important than others. The inability to name the landscape has, in the past, worked to make me feel displaced from it.

I think about how, growing up, English dominated Arabic. How many of my ancestral traditions were overwritten, and how I have worked to reclaim them, coming to terms with all that I will never retrieve. The afterlives of colonialism live on in all of these languages and how they are lost.

Today, I am a figure oriented toward sprawling green, toward water, toward the horizon line craning its neck through a cloudy morning. I pay attention to what is tangible and sensorial. Perhaps this exercise isn't at all about the ability or inability to name the trees, but rather an acceptance of letting go of nomenclature. We have disguised our trees in colonial replacements, and my tongue subconsciously resists.

Restalrig Railway Path / 'heatwave'

I'm going out for a run on the path nearby. I've only just taken up running and I'm still very slow. But this season has taught me that I hold fear in my body. I hold anger, exhaustion and melancholy in my body. There is something building up inside me and calcifying into a hardness that I'm afraid is becoming unmovable. Permanent. I can feel anxiety spread through my limbs, depositing uncertainty into every crevice. And when done with my literal body, anxiety finds its way into my dreams, into my dream-body, bringing together the real and unreal in an eddying haze.

It feels sometimes impossible to go through the motions of daily life: an egg boiling almost silently in a pot of water, morning prayers followed by a lukewarm shower – because in this building the water never really gets hot – and a scroll through my notifications to catch up on conversations from a time zone seven hours away. With growing concern, I feel like I am slowly adapting to constant unease. Lately, I have been waking up feeling agitated. Nervous. Confounded in and by my own skin. The feeling lingers until it's the constant sensation of light but also persistent numbness.

In *Threads*, the poet and academic Sandeep Parmar asks: how do poets of colour 'embody the "I"?' and this question easily becomes one of the nodes of my green project. My life here in Scotland stretches out before me as my feet thud against the concrete. My path here unravels like the longest line of a poem, where sometimes words extend just far enough away that they give off the impression of being isolated from the rest of the text – isolated and alone.

/

This morning, a week of rain has cleared up. The sky is a daguerreotype and the sun is bright white exposure. Across the Atlantic, my mother has been tending to her garden in the front yard of my old home. This is a new pastime of hers. Growing up, we didn't plant flowers or spend time in gardens. I remember the duplex we rented when I was eight years old had a backyard with an impressive crab-apple tree in the middle. Its tart green fruit would drop heavily and land in the dirt below, left to rot into the ground before the cycle began again. The grass around the tree was overgrown, and there was an unmanicured rose bush near our fence that was dense with bees. All of this was right outside our walls, and still, we rarely touched it. The lush backyard might as well have been a separate world.

The day is hotter than I expect. I put away the photo of ellipsoidal pink flowers, feeling a twinge of loneliness mixing with pricks of heat. I imagine my mother across the ocean, wearing her sunglasses, digging her hands into the dirt, and changing ever so slightly as each day passes. I want to know this version of her, the woman whose hectic and unrelenting job as a retail manager has changed somewhat, just as most things have during this pandemic. I want to know her as the soil-stricken woman she's become. And simultaneously, I worry about her health: she is someone who is immunocompromised. Her job at the dollar store makes her an essential worker, and when she video calls me from the back storeroom, I stare intently at her blue mask, making sure it's fitted tightly over her mouth and nose. I tell her when it isn't.

/

It's time to run again and I can already feel beads of sweat collecting at my body's joints. The world sizzles under sharp sunlight. Today, *bulbul calling* is an archive of this smoke. The poem 'heatwave' opens with the line,

I am writing for you.

It is as if this collection of poems understands my sudden loneliness. Living away from the touchstones of family and tradition, living as a tiny unit with just my partner, I fear I'm becoming normalised to Scotland's particular brand of whiteness. I ask myself, *when was the last time I heard my family speaking in Kutchi?* I worry that after this time of stark isolation, I won't be able to understand my first language with the same fluency as even just a year ago.

I feel like the thread once tied to an already ephemeral kind of self-understanding is being worn away without my noticing.

/

First, I read 'heatwave' as an invitation. Then I think of it as a lament for something. This journey is for *you*, says Pratyusha. The oleander plant within the poem reaches toward me, wild and eerie outside of its verse. What has the poet given up to be here with me, on the Restalrig Railway Path, as I dislodge the creeping build-up? The body is so very good at collecting, and then it is so very good at adapting around the fissures and shapes made from its gathering. As my feet smack hard against the ground, the edges of the world blur on either side of me.

What have I asked the environment to give up so I can, myself, be here to witness its heavy heat and its constant withering?

Assimilation is an empty field

I'm struck by the allusion to all that has been lost in this poem. I'm stirred by how author and reader, Pratyusha and myself together, in the brevity of this line, embody the empty field. I feel like I am losing something even beyond language itself. I've noticed my memories of Alberta are wearing away. They are overrun with gaps and missing sections. It's like when our eyes are deprived of light and we experience phosphenes, those evasive flashes of colour. What I struggle to remember oscillates between sharp, bright bursts of light and changing tones of eigengrau in perfect darkness.

/

Just ahead is a railway bridge. In a moment, I'll run underneath it and then emerge on the other side. But for now, I read 'heatwave' on *this* side, amongst what I know. Wildflowers brush up against my ankles and slip through my reality. I think of how reading a poem is like walking through a portal or crossing a bridge, a linking of one memory to another.

Our bodies hold unfathomable movement – so much of it symbolic, ancestral, passed down – and we constantly seek out other worlds. Sometimes we emerge onto the empty field, into deep dissatisfaction and in ruins.

Lighthouses

Where land and water meet

Autumn

The light was almost perfect and the wind was still. It felt unlike Scotland on the cusp of December as I knew it, usually overcast and bone-chilling. Last week's snow had melted and still-drying leaves rustled in the verge. I unbuttoned my coat at the neck and took off my gloves. I appreciated the slow ripple of my hair when my head turned to look out at the harbour, glad that it wasn't, for once, wind-stricken and tangled into knots by the Scottish gales.

I was walking down Pier Place in Newhaven close to sundown, marvelling at the lavender cast on the water, when I caught a glimpse of a lighthouse from afar. At the end of the eastern breakwater of the harbour, now used mostly for pleasure craft, the octagonal tower was stalwart, blunt and sure of itself. An airy cloud corkscrewed toward it. It looked like a feathery lightning bolt. The lighthouse was dramatic and beautiful in its isolation, fifty feet tall and white except for its dusty-pink base. First lit in 1878, then decommissioned in 1930, the Newhaven Harbour Lighthouse represents a time of expansion when the pier was extended and heightened. It replaced – and subsequently was also itself eventually replaced by – a different lighthouse.

I felt compelled toward it, having always been drawn to lighthouses and their representations, their romanticised entities. *The lonely tower at the edge of the sea.* Somewhere in that mythology, I saw myself. A lighthouse was a strange man-made object that lived at the boundary line where land and water meet. From the shoreland, a lighthouse signalled the oncoming appearance of water. From the water, the lighthouse was an important marker of land. In that murky middle space, choreographed light would shine in its own unique pattern. Then and there, at Newhaven, I couldn't help but walk toward it, reminded of the memories I have of different lighthouses on different coasts.

By chance, I had been reading about illuminance – the amount of light a source emits – on *Radicle*, one of my favourite newsletters on decolonising the outdoors. It had slipped into my inbox that morning; intrigued, I later found a chart that compared typical 'lux levels' of various places. Understanding lux levels helps us to know how bright a space is, and devices called illuminance meters are used to measure the amount of light that falls on a surface, translating what seems utterly ungraspable into a numerical value.

Different miasmas of light make me feel different things. All my life, I have measured light, illuminance, by way of gut feeling such as reverence or fear. Light is intrinsically linked with my faith. There is a passage in the Quran I return to, and in English, the only language I read, it partly translates to *Allah is the light of the heavens and the earth.* In Annie Dillard's essay 'Total Eclipse', light is philosophical, almost revelatory, and the lack of it is as awesome as it is terrible.

British summer sunshine has a lux level of 50,000. I wondered how that compared to Calgary summer sunshine, Calgary being one of the sunniest, brightest places I have ever lived. This number is a huge contrast to even a well-lit office, where the lux level is only 500. *Radicle* emphasised that even on an overcast day, grey and gloomy, the intensity of light was still much higher outdoors than indoors. The graph I looked at suggested an overcast day could have a lux level of anywhere between 1,000 to 5,000.

The relativity of these numbers is clear. My fold-out desk in my bedroom at home, though facing the window, will never come close to the light exposure of stepping outside and tilting my face upward toward the sky.

That afternoon, when I encountered the Newhaven Lighthouse, I was in high spirits. I had just visited Coburg House's biannual open art studios. It was a rare pleasure, walking into a studio and seeing each artist's tools alongside their work. From portraiture to landscape, metalwork to crochet, cyanotype to sculpture, the experience left me feeling abuzz with the prospect of creation, the infinite possibility of making.

I was reminded of the charged space that spreads out wide in front of a person once they find their voice, their own exquisite means of expression. I flipped gently through artists' books on display and eyed sketches of nascent works. A work-in-progress piece drew me in when I saw crimson paint and gold-leaf foil on an otherwise bare canvas. I understood then how little I knew about this artist's medium, shocked that the gold came first. I was enamoured by the lightly drawn figure within it, a barely there draft of a woman's body, lines disappearing against the intensity of her elaborate, filled-in skirt.

At the studios, I purchased a handmade cyanotype printed notebook by the artist Maria Vigers. It was stitched with teal thread. I ran my fingers over the jagged, almost haphazard pattern, my favourite part of the whole artefact. *this too is a glistening*, the collaborative writing project I'd worked on with my friends Nina Mingya Powles, Jessica J. Lee and Pratyusha, had only come out a few days earlier. My friends had spent hours folding then binding our books together with forest-green thread and, when I received my copy, I marvelled at the silken feel of it. In fact, I noticed the knot had come undone where the thread looped through the pages in the middle and I retied it carefully. I loved this detail, the slight unravelling of an artisanal, handmade thing. I loved that I could imagine the maker's deft fingers – in this case someone close to me – sewing the book together in the autumnal light of her home near Epping Forest.

I thought it must have been a confluence of the fresh, crisping light at Newhaven Harbour and my closeness to artmaking that filled me with elation at the pier. I had otherwise spent the week indoors, grappling with a sadness that had been pulled open by a recent writing project that navigated Edinburgh's colonial history. Beyond that, I had hidden myself away in the dark corners of my home, coming to terms with my father's latest hospital visit. As I sunk further into my melancholy, a deep pool that I found myself wading into more and more often, I found it increasingly hard to muster the will to even get dressed, to leave the house at all. But that day, unexpectedly, I encountered joy at the sight of a lighthouse, feeling small and warm and safe next to it. As if it had promised and delivered guidance to an enclosed comfort, a momentary sanctuary.

And I thought it could have been the light, spearing through the gentle cloudscape, that unfurled this sudden happiness. It could have been, too, the rough ridges of teal thread I continued to swipe my fingers over, as if strumming an instrument. Light – lightness – and art, together.

Scientific devices and genuine physics aside, I try to imagine the lux level of artistic sensibility. Not of the studio itself, but the act of creation that happens within. I think of the overhanging bulbs reflecting off gold-leaf panels, pleating down drawings of kimono-inspired clothing. The two-dimensional fabrics draping across the canvas, ablaze and luminescent, the woman's etched lines held inside.

Light is considered the dominant zeitgeber, or environmental cue, influencing our sleep-wake cycle. For much of autumn, I spent my time indoors, reluctant to leave my home. I found myself awake early, at five or six in the morning. I absorbed the blue light of my phone, which I kept underneath my pillow so I could check messages from my family at any hour. One day, I caught the tail end of a conversation between my mother and sisters from a time zone seven hours away. Through jumbled texts, I gleaned that my father had gone missing in the night, his items scattered all across the floor, the lights still on, the front door unlocked. I scrolled down the chat quickly, saw that he had eventually been found, breathed out in relief.

In 'The Anthropology of Water', Anne Carson describes how, when her father first showed signs of illness, she began to wake earlier and earlier in the morning. The body seemed to react before the mind knew how to. With dread, I watched as early mornings grew darker into late autumn. And as I worked, my writing slow, shapeless and filled with ennui, I moved a desk lamp close to my notebook. The yellow light reflected against the near-blackness of those early hours. I squinted out the window, my chest tight. What did my body use to feel like, without this hard carapace of anxiety?

It feels too simple to say light makes me happier. But perhaps articulation is not the point and the body is. There is an instinctual pattern incited by the process of light entering the retina and entraining what I learn is called the suprachiasmatic nucleus – the circadian pacemaker. When I learn that circadian rhythms have oscillations of approximately twenty-four hours, adjusting minutely to the moving earth across seasons, I think to myself I would like to write a poem reflecting, somehow, this rhythm.

Winter

On the shortest day of the year, we woke up before sunrise in a shared dormitory at Tossals Verds in Mallorca. We moved around quietly, trying not to disturb anyone, even though this was the most rural, and hence the emptiest, refugi on the GR 221 route. Besides us and the hostel keeper, the dormitory housed two young women who'd travelled together and arrived shortly before we did.

The night before, the four of us sat at wooden tables near the fire and chatted intermittently in-between reading novels. One of the other hikers asked if we had ever stayed in a bothy, a type of rudimentary shelter scattered across rural Scotland that is traditionally open and free for travellers to use. She was keen to visit the Highlands and stay in one. That was the gist of our conversation; we drank café con leche and spoke about our favourite long walks, or those walks we hoped we could one day take.

I didn't reveal that I wasn't sure what a bothy was like. I had never stayed in one. The GR 221 route is a strenuous, difficult trail, and it was an ambitious endeavour for me to undertake, probably right at the height of my abilities. I felt like an imposter as the others talked knowingly; they were seasoned adventurers, fit and fearless. I had started on this multi-day hike with the hope of understanding more about the world and about myself, of finding peace or something like it in the long kilometres travelled. I generally tried not to fool myself into thinking of nature as a lasting salve or a cure-all for my creeping depression. But at the hostel, drinking coffee with thrill seekers, I acquiesced that for me, this trek *was* a search for self, for purpose at a time when I was feeling displaced from family, from my religion, and from who I was. I wanted to relearn how to love a world that hurt, and through that, to hopefully relearn how to love myself – this new version of me that succumbed so easily to sadness.

T and I had already hiked for two full days around the Tramuntana Mountains, passing olive groves and limestone walls. We had arrived at the hostel situated at the foot of the Tossals Verds massif with sore bodies. Our descent of the mountain had been steep, dotted with spry mountain goats that easily meandered the path.

Our map showed that of all the places we were to stay, this refugi was the area furthest inland, the furthest away from the coast. Deep greens guided us down: juniper, oak, citrus and almond.

Hovering at the forefront of my mind was the thought that, the next morning, we would have to get back onto the main trail. This required taking the same path again, but hiking uphill. At the hostel, my legs were heavy as I moved up and down the stairs, and my shoulders ached from carrying everything on my back. These physical pains made me notice my limbs and muscles in new ways, how they throbbed as I lay down to sleep, stiffness growing in places I otherwise forgot were there – as if ordinarily, when not twinging with discomfort, though that in itself was rare, my body was an amorphous thing. I massaged my calves, thinking of how we were only a third of our way into our hike, with four more days of walking ahead of us. Our next stop was Sóller, the municipality on the northwest coast. We would be staying at another hostel near the town, one that was right next to a lighthouse.

In the 1980s, the poet Anne Carson went on a pilgrimage in Spain and later wrote that some pilgrimages were conducted 'in the belief that question can travel into answer as water into thirst'. To travel to Sóller, to reach our own holy site – Far des Cap Gros, the still-shining lighthouse that marked our destination – was in itself a kind of pilgrimage. Over the last two days, my mind was cracked open under the towering mountains and their vast shadows. I attended to everything I could, trying to notice it all, as if the island held the clues to my happiness and even the map back to my lost spirituality. It was as if I thought I could find the truth of my ebbing faith nested within the stone and there uncover a steadfast belief that would ultimately lead to solace. Perhaps these steps would jostle something free from my heart, just as seeing the yawing sky meet the humbling ocean from such a high altitude released my awe. It was a sight that made me feel, once again, like praying – a ritual I had recently stopped and found difficult to retrieve again.

A few years ago, two of my cousins made the Hajj pilgrimage to Mecca and walked in the footsteps of Prophet Muhammad. Though all Muslims are required to undertake this pilgrimage at least once, if financially and physically able to do so, this was the first time that anyone close to me had made the journey. They stopped to gaze at the Ka'ba, a sacred space of unity and monotheism, in the courtyard of the Grand Mosque. Its cuboid structure was covered in black and gold embroidered cloth. Amidst the drone of voices and flurry of bodies, they circled the Ka'ba counterclockwise seven times while reciting prayers. I thought of how firm their belief was, how dedicated their devotion to Allah, to have joined the throng of pilgrims and drawn meaning from such an experience. I desired even a modicum of that peace, of that unwavering faith.

I knew I wanted too much. I was led by a fierce longing to overcome my mind and my body, or to exhaust it into compliance. 'Pilgrims were people who figured things out as they walked,' writes Carson. Each step forward felt like progress toward the unknown thing that would heal me, heal my mind; an unravelling of the knot that had seized my body over time.

In the morning, we slipped on our hiking clothes in the darkness. Having brought so little with us, we tucked our belongings inside our packs easily and left the building with still-bleary eyes. I was wearing my grey windbreaker when we began the uphill climb. Without the sun, the late December weather felt brisk on our faces. Behind us, the stones of Tossals Verds Refugi slowly disappeared into the rocky landscape, nestled deeply in the forest. All we could see as we left were the bright orange lights at its front door.

The island of Mallorca averages three hundred days of sunlight a year. As we climbed, the darkness crept into twilight with the sun still loosely held beneath the horizon and its light diffusing into shades of blues across the sky. A thin band of orange formed behind the jutting mountain range, shining behind a distinctive flat-topped butte. Eventually, all the rock faces to the east were awash in the vibrant tint of sunrise. The clouds looked soft and pink around us.

We paused cliffside and admired the sunrise as it spilled out from the valley, Tossals Verds Refugi a tiny, invisible dot somewhere amidst the shimmering flora. It felt good to stop, to cast eyes on how the burgeoning sun painted the Mallorcan landscape. I tried my best to notice how the mountain range compared to the Albertan Rockies. Its grasses and shrubs were attuned to this different, hotter climate, the same climate that made sweat drip down my neck and drench my hair until it was a shiny black. As we looked around us, I thought this was what I was here for, what I wanted all along to experience: the beautiful world. A new perspective that I could then take forward in my life.

The GR 221 is called La Ruta de Pedra en Sec, or the route of the dry-stone walls. It's around one hundred and fifty kilometres of hiking across seven or so stages. Because much of the Serra Tramuntana is privately owned, the trails themselves can change at the discretion of the landowners, and waymarking is available only when on the public paths. Over the course of our trip, we got lost often in those long stretches without signposting, squinting into the distance and looking for some other traveller's cairn to guide us. Once, we ended up traversing for an hour down the wrong narrow path, which tapered off into a menacing cliff. I stared down at the chasm below, my heart thumping at the height of the drop, our destination visible but impossible to get to from that vantage point.

When we mapped out our six-day route along the natural stone walls that gave La Ruta de Pedra en Sec its name, we chose to start at the north of the island. That morning, on our third day, we left before sunrise. We knew that the hike between Tossals Verds and Sóller was the longest of them all and we were racing daylight; the sun would be up for just over nine hours. Not including stops, the guides estimated eight hours of walking, and I suspected I walked slower than the average GR 221 hiker.

The holm oak trees provided some shade and shelter as we continued our walk under the risen sun. Holm oaks are representative of the Mediterranean, able to withstand drought and grow at altitudes of up to fourteen hundred metres. I often stopped beneath them, letting my heart rate slow next to their greyish trunks, this reprieve yet another of my extractions from the land. The pause allowed me to rein in my thoughts, my mind having wandered during stretches of silence as we walked. The long silences, aside from our footsteps or the bleating of small animals, along with the afternoon heat, dislodged strange memories and the impressions of otherwise forgotten dreams.

'The mind is also a landscape of sorts,' writes author and activist Rebecca Solnit. 'Walking is one way to traverse it.' I thought about my family, who I hadn't seen for so long. I thought about the wrench of trauma, how it forked my life into before and after. When I grew tired of thinking and remembering, I found myself repeating song lyrics. My mind would quieten then and I was relieved, letting my taut anxiety loosen into a kind of numbness. For a long part of that day, I had Mitski's 'Heat Lightning' stuck in my head. The haunting melody and its crescendo swept into the dramatic landscape, my mind repeating the words *I surrender*.

We eventually reached an artificial canal and walked alongside it for several kilometres. It took a very long time. I felt that this was one of the characteristics that tipped our walk over the threshold into something spiritual, into something physiologically and emotionally *more*. It was almost monotonous and, in the monotony, was pleasure. I thought of the poet and essayist Mary Oliver, for whom walking in nature was a tenet of its own kind: 'I walk, all day, across the heaven-verging field.' Even this part of our pilgrimage, without the fluorescent sunrise or gratifying steep ascent to remind us of our wonder, felt purposeful in its flatness. It felt evocative, like it could mean something to keep going and to know that, eventually, I would arrive as a different version of myself.

We peered over the edge of the aqueduct at leaves and acorns spinning down the lithe expanse of water. This was the island's water supply, and we followed it to Reservoir Cúber, the view of the lake at last stealing the measured rhythm of our attention. And sensations came all at once then; the vast lake view, impressive and quenching like an oasis; the black vulture high up in the sky, tilting its body and then gliding fast in the wind; the new shade of green, similar to sated moss in a wetland. During our walk along the canal, dense clouds had started to hang over the horizon, but at the reservoir, blue sky broke through.

We were heading steadily, if not quickly, to Far des Cap Gros, the lighthouse right next to Refugi de Muleta. It was still hours away, but glancing at the sky and at the pouring light, we felt invincible, like we had all the time in the world. Reaching Cúber was its own satisfying arrival, and under the soaring birds, again in the realm of dry-stone walls, we sat and ate a late lunch. Afterward, climbing again, the flatness of the aqueduct long gone and replaced with the familiar swell of mountains, I saw, at last, a wide and clear view of the sea from above. And, zooming in on my camera, there it was: a white pillar cutting into the sky. The lighthouse perched on the headland. I thought us nearly there, seeing it jutting out proudly from the cliffside, and I wish I could have known then how far away it still was.

Far des Cap Gros is on the furthest end of the bay, which was once a military telegraph station. The official trail signs estimated that the lighthouse was about an hour and a half walking distance from Sóller. When we reached the picturesque town, we took a break on a bench next to La Iglesia de Sant Bartomeu, a remarkable church of modernist architecture with a handsome rose window. The sculptural trees in the middle of the square shivered in the wind, which was picking up slightly. It was late afternoon when we felt the first few raindrops fall and saw dark wet spots scatter onto the stone at our feet.

The cobblestones were sleek as we followed them out of the town and back to the weathered trail. Along the way, we caught sight of shiny-leafed citrus trees, oranges and lemons glowing from within assemblages of bright green. And just beyond the terraced gardens, where fruit trees were welcoming and abundant, we saw the mountain pass draped with dark rain-clouds and a thick mist. When we looked back, the details of the elaborate municipality of Sóller were softened into a blur, as if it was a mirage whose time was up, as if it was on the brink of vanishing.

We were too slow in the rain. Puddles formed in shallow pools, divots filling quickly with water across the trail. What had been hard and mostly packed dirt gave way to mud and slippery stones. The light waned and evening came at once, turning the sky blue. I only marvelled for a brief moment at how the sky looked just like earlier that morning, but in reverse, the colours of the day seeping out of view and leaving darkness in their wake.

We had hiked from before sunrise to after sunset. I thought it sounded romantic, but learned rapidly that, in reality, it was dangerous. The unseen stones seemed to become more jagged and larger, like small boulders. I wasn't sure if their growth was a fact or if it was made true by my fear. We stepped over them cautiously at first, but as the rain grew harder and our surroundings darker, we found ourselves slipping haphazardly over and between them, our hiking boots losing grip and sinking into streaming water that had once been a firm and dry path.

When the lighthouse came into view, I felt my hammering chest slow down. I made a sound that was a cross between relief and agony. For Rebecca Solnit, 'walking, ideally, is a state in which the mind, the body, and the world are aligned' and, in that respect, I thought my pilgrimage over. I was unaligned with the dark world, interiorly uneven and as chipped as the stones at my feet. I didn't pray to Allah but cursed Them, though not more than I cursed myself for believing I could succeed on this walk. For making myself believe I wanted to hike the dry-stone route at all.

The lighthouse emitted three white flashes, a total of fifteen seconds per cycle. We gradually made our way over the wet trail, and the storm pummelled us as we walked. The lighthouse's lamp flickered by again and again, cutting through the dark corridor of trees that enclosed us. Soon our guiding light became a pattern in the background, bright, shining, but seemingly not getting any closer. It was then I realised that it was not enough to see light. Finding light wasn't the end of the journey.

I suddenly stopped and keeled over, my breath coming out in sharp exhales, my chest feeling somehow both too tight and like it might overfill with blood and shatter. Dread came over me like a dark shroud. T shone his phone light at me in concern, noticing the deep swell and shudder of my breath, my irregularly timed gasps for air that never seemed to fill my lungs. I felt it, then, creeping up over my body. I saw it in the murky tendrils that escaped from the gleaming rocks and entered my airway, my throat closing around them. I thought I was dying. I could no longer feel or control my body, because I was sure my body was no longer there. I couldn't move.

'Pilgrimage is a kind of freedom that is also a sort of bondage, because when you undertake a pilgrimage, you're bound to everything about the road.' Anne Carson said this decades after she wrote about her pilgrimage in *Plainwater*, reflecting on the experience during a talk for undergraduates at NYU.

The lighthouse kept flickering its light in groups of three, in its fifteen-second pattern. It did this for the entire duration of my panic attack. The phone light intermingled with its flashing. When I returned to my body and to the present tense, only minutes later, I felt something in me shift. What should have been a guiding light had become almost taunting, a trigger. To come close. To never arrive. To be reminded so jarringly of my brokenness, which I had travelled all this way to escape.

Although we made it to the Refugi de Muleta eventually, in the pitch-black of night, soaking wet, I think a part of me stayed there, near the lighthouse tower, in the rocky outcrop awash with rain. When she wrote about Heptonstall, scholar and writer Emily Van Duyne called it a grey stone tower. 'You could let down your hair,' she writes; 'the rain would lash it to the stones, and there, like lichen, it would stay.' I was bound to this pilgrimage, both to the love it refused to unearth and to the changed self that emerged from it. My hair wet with rain, my body hollowed by fear, my reverence transfigured into a new distrust of the light.

Spring

I grew up in a place far away from the ocean. Alberta is a landlocked province with no officially maintained lighthouses. There are a few buildings that stand next to its navigable waters, like Sylvan Lake, but it's not a place I associate with the mythology of tall glowing towers beside the wild sea. When I think of my hometown, I picture the boreal forest, creeping treelines, glacial paths embedded into rock, deep snow and black ice. I think of headlights and long drives rather than vessels that move across great waters. I think of deer with shining eyes plucking leaves from the university gardens, bobcats making headlines on community noticeboards, flat prairies where you can see ahead for miles and miles, and dry grass flickering back and forth in the wind, its movements on an entirely different scale than ocean waves.

I think about this as I lean my head against the seat on the number twenty-six bus. It takes five minutes to walk from my front door to the Abbeyhill stop, where I catch the bus going east. And from there, it takes what feels like only minutes to arrive at the coast. The reality of Alberta, dry and flat and sprawling, feels far from here, from Scotland, where I have easy access to the water. I can't imagine otherwise now, my hair and skin accustomed to the humid climate, my swimsuit always tucked into the bottom of my bag in case I decide to swim in the Firth of Forth, cold water that comes in from the North Sea.

Sara Ahmed writes that a nation is a constructed familiar space, and I've become crosshatched with familiarities and unfamiliarities over my lifetime. With each year away from Alberta, I become more keenly aware of the mixing and mingling of who I am, of my constant hybridisation. There are parts of my Canadian identity that have frayed at the edges or otherwise unravelled to become entwined with my identity in Scotland. In *Ban en Banlieue*, Bhanu

Kapil reflects on the paradigms of the immigrant, who is from elsewhere, and the monster, who assimilates or else thrives in their difference. As I collect the fibres of different places, my mind crammed with knowledges and discrepancies, I increasingly feel strung in-between them, these identities that mirror one another but depend largely on the gaze placed upon them.

And I realise I also leave imprints on places. In *States of the Body Produced by Love*, Nisha Ramayya writes that the goddess 'Mātaṅgī crosses boundaries' and 'wherever she roams becomes slick with the feel of her'. As I cross these real and imagined boundaries and feel slick with the land memories and sensations between them, they are becoming slick with me too. The sea leaves its map all over me and, in return, my steps become visible whorls on the wet sand.

Where Alberta has very few standing lighthouses, Scotland has a rich and enthralling history when it comes to these buildings. I learn this by accident at first, while reading about other lighthouses further from home, and then I can't help but dive into the literature around it. When I tell friends that I've been reading about Scottish lighthouses, everyone seems to have their own story about a favourite one that means something to them. And there are many to choose from, more than two hundred different beacons across the country. They are emblematic, one of this country's heirlooms. Lighthouses draw in the imagination and allow us our in-between dreams. Perched on headlands, on cliffs, and overlooking mesmerising waters, they are perfect metaphors for our human tendency toward liminality, our identities and homes that never feel fixed or placed, whether our histories are ribbed with elsewheres or we fill our dreams with future journeys.

When I think about these lonely towers dotting the Scottish coastline, I imagine dark, overcast skies and dangerous weather looming over seaside towns. Edinburgh is itself often overcast. My first photographs of the city from a visit in 2016 show glistening cobblestones and heavy blue evening light; behind my silhouette are brazen clouds thick on the horizon, or wind caught on film through the trembling of oak trees and silver birch. Wet, gothic architecture and slippery stone buildings stole my attention and, within months, I packed two suitcases and moved here.

In my reading, I come across the artist J.M.W. Turner's depiction of Bell Rock, Scotland's oldest surviving rock lighthouse. The illustration, watercolour and gouache with scratching out on paper, shows the lighthouse being battered by a storm and ships with tall masts tilting ominously toward the waves. They are close, those ships, to the lighthouse and to the rock underneath it, which is only uncovered at low water. It is a scene that visually captures the threshold that fascinates me, the two different states embodied by the symbol of the lighthouse: land and water.

The bus reaches our stop and T and I disembark in a small mining town on the east coast. Our plan is to walk along the shoreline from Prestonpans to North Berwick with an overnight stop at Gullane Beach. Before this trip, our two-man tent had been dormant in our little storage cupboard. It had been long enough for me to forget the hard work involved in camping, the sometimes sleepless nights of burrowing deep into my thermal sleeping bag, wrapped up in scarves and borrowed hoodies, in the foothills of Kananaskis or the snow-crowned mountains of Banff. I linger instead on my memories of rainfall on the tent's surface, one of my favourite sounds, then zipping open the storm flaps to watch the morning sun stream against the wet landscape afterward.

Part of our walk crosses the John Muir Way, a trail that traverses central Scotland from coast to coast. We hike through long stretches of beach, with views of the roiling waters, past Seton Sands and the nature reserve at Aberlady. It's spring, so the scores of pink-footed geese that hail from Iceland and overrun the bay in autumn are gone now. I've seen them before, once with T's parents and his aunt, all avid birdwatchers who stood enrapt underneath the flocks of geese that swarmed across the sky.

The sea along the Scottish coast is rough and we choose to walk close to the water, climbing over sand dunes against a blistering wind. The shoreline is bleak, but I think it's also atmospheric with rocks and weeds jutting out for mere seconds before being thrashed by water and sinking below the surface of the sea again. And the wind, muscular gales that I have come to associate so strongly with my home in Scotland, picks up the sand too. Its top layers are ushered around the shore, crafting attractive, eerie patterns that point in the direction of the wind like a compass as wide as a landscape. It makes the earth beneath us feel like it is moving and unstable. It quivers in air that mimics water.

In 1880, the Scottish novelist Robert Louis Stevenson wrote, 'Whenever I smell salt water, I know that I am not far from one of the works of my ancestors.' It thrills me to know that the lighthouses I grow obsessed with are part of a writer's legacy. The fact is magnetic. I delve into biographies and archival material about the Stevensons and the work they achieved in making the treacherous seas around Scotland more navigable with light. I can't help but think that my ancestors, too, were from places that emanated with saltwater. They also navigated harsh weather – monsoons – and the wild currents of meeting seas in order to engineer their lives. Landlocked, with its streaming, beautiful prairies, Alberta is, after all, only one of my inheritances, only one headland of the many that I'm suspended between.

As soon as I begin to look, the history is ubiquitous and, in fact, unavoidable. On the Scottish island of Islay, I was once part of a nature poetry walk in Portnahaven. It took place in collaboration with a volunteer from the Islay Natural History Trust, who identified the flora and fauna as we walked along the Port Weymss path. Our route overlooked the sea, which I remember as both terrifying and welcoming in that uncanny and mercurial way of expansive water. I thought I could see where the tides became dangerous, strong and unmanageable. The smell of the sea and its salt was palpable as I read my watery poems. H, the volunteer, pointed out seals on the far end of the coast and spoke to us about the forced Clearances that dwindled Islay's population; politics and nature as inextricably intertwined. Some months later, I learned from a friend that the Rhinns of Islay Lighthouse, the unwavering landmark of our walk, is also known as a Stevenson Lighthouse, having been designed by Robert Stevenson.

At Gullane, the unruly sand and tumultuous waters even out into soft golden shores. By the time we arrive, there are already kite surfers and dog walkers enjoying the beach. We set up camp within the privacy of a gathering of trees, then take our books with us to the shoreline to enjoy the vistas as we read. Scotland's culture of wild camping near its eastern shores is, of course, different from Alberta's mountainous national parks. But I am comforted by how similar the serenity feels even if the scenes are different. The mixing and mingling, the unpinnable quality of who I am and who I feel like, fades away from crisis and into gentle understanding.

The last leg of our walk takes us to North Berwick. It's almost entirely sea level, though the beaches get rockier as we move further away from Gullane. Eventually, as we make our way down the wavering coastline, Fidra Island comes into view. It's only a few hundred yards off the mainland. This island houses its own Stevenson lighthouse, too – which is no surprise, I think now. Robert Louis Stevenson himself wrote that 'all the sea lights in Scotland are signed with our name'. As we near the end of our walk, the Fidra Lighthouse guides our way. It's seventeen metres tall, engineered by Thomas and David A. Stevenson, and we see small specks, seabirds, circling it as we move across, two people threaded in the liminality of our own journeys. I think of the ghosts housed in its yellow-painted gallery and black lantern house. I think of the history that pours out with ferocity into the sea, before collapsing onto the shore and into our lives.

Summer

In a way, poetry has taught me a lot about loneliness.

Sometimes I think the more I give to the page, the less I have available for the people around me, even the people I love. When I write about my ancestors, their voices become woven with my own. Slowly, almost imperceptibly, these crafted versions start to overtake already indistinct shapes until the once real memory is a rendition of my own face. As I pour myself into a poem like this, language helps me excavate myself for myself. But I'm noticing that in a strange and unexpected way, language doubly becomes a wall between myself and others. Because I manipulate it into a deliberately crafted object, language forecloses any real intimacy. Instead, I end up further entrenched in my own secluded interiority, nestling into that space and maybe eventually disappearing there.

My thoughts about art and loneliness permeate the summer months. I'm visiting Oregon in early July a decade after I lived there, and it's the lighthouses on the Pacific Coast that I'm drawn to revisiting the most. I want to see as many of them as possible, and I try to understand the origins of this strong pull. In her book *On Lighthouses*, Jazmina Barrera writes magnetically about her affinity for them. 'It's perhaps true that I like lighthouses because I am disoriented,' she says. 'I always feel as if I'm adrift.' I relate to dwelling within those pressing forces of feeling adrift. I think

I see the lighthouse and its guiding light as the fastener of an in-between space. It's also a clear, resplendent symbol of isolation, often perched alone on headlands or on islands, or even on sea-submerged rocks that themselves seem adrift in a large breadth of water. My growing feelings of loneliness seem to want to house in the theory and imagery that surrounds the figure of the lighthouse. In this resolute symbol of self-imposed exile.

That morning, to get to Heceta Head Lighthouse, an iconic emblem on the Pacific Coast, I choose the path that is part of the Oregon Coast Trail. It offers striking views to the shores of Hobbit Beach below. This is a part of the coast that I have walked many times before, sometimes taking the longer Ponsler Way that moves through immense areas of unrelenting beach before giving way to the woods over the course of a day. Today, though, I feel like retreating into myself and I desire shortcuts to everything. My mood is at odds with the brightness of the very early morning, where the tall trunks of trees cluster together like magnificent towers themselves, the sun spearing through them and draping the trail in golden light.

I have been reading about tree species that were brought to Scotland from Oregon in the nineteenth century, introduced by foresters who planted them in compact plantations. Some Scottish glens have formed functioning ecosystems that resemble those in the Pacific Northwest, and that thought engraves itself into my mind. I'm not sure where I, myself, fall on that spectrum. After years away from North America, years I have spent blossoming up the Scottish hillsides, I find myself considering whether I am an ecosystem that more resembles here or there.

I think that the evergreens might be Douglas firs, with their brazen verticality. These are a type of pine tree rather than a true fir. But I learn along the way that they are mostly Sitka spruce, and where they are densely packed, even when bathed in the sun, it is extremely dark in the thickets. I notice the shapes of their trunks, how some trees wind around others, or look inextricable from the licorice ferns that hang onto them. A placard calls these *twisted trees*, with a further description that seems to reflect myself back at me: 'a tree's location helps determine its shape.'

I think writing poetry allows me to shape-shift the truth of myself and that is part of why it is so alluring. Sometimes I relish the fact that I can bring something so specific into existence, the same as a sculptor or a painter. This carries with it the acute pleasure and satisfaction of craftsmanship. Poetry is a relationship of its own: it requires time, a level of sincerity and deliberate care. Recently, for me, it has also been tied closely to grief, both in terms of process and subject matter. I have found myself lingering in my own felt tensions of authenticity, in the sense that through my work, which takes up long stretches of my day, I can distract someone from who I really am and what I really feel with metaphor. I think more frequently now about how, when I create something new, I am creating something deliberately artificial in many ways.

Poets are builders and the outpouring is not necessarily always the point. Sometimes, I aim to write a beautiful, precise, technically sound object rather than live in the therapeutic outcome. In fact, my best poems, I think, are not the ones that expose raw parts of myself within them. They are the ones that reflect a reader back to themselves, driving new or transformed understandings of the world because of a skilful metonymic flow and the delicate handling of imagination. But I think this distance, too, contributes to loneliness. I want my poems to be experience rather than spectacle, but I don't want to lose the raw truth of myself either.

The first viewpoint is awash in a scattering of spruce trees and rhododendrons that, as I walk closer to the edge of the cliff, give way to the sight of welcoming waters. This stop is about a kilometre into the hike, where after a series of switchbacks, the view opens up to the north. It's so quiet below, under the rustle of windblown branches, and the beach is devoid of any footprints. Just soaring birds – mostly large gulls, but a hawk or vulture at times as well. The lighthouse is not yet in view, but I sense it is close.

Before going to Oregon, I had told friends that I was *hiding away* for the summer. I apologised for my absence with the explanation that I was trying to respect the limits of my mind and my body, but I think it was more than that. I was wilfully pulling away, letting myself retreat, and getting into reclusive habits that I was unwilling to try and break. I was in a state of hopelessness. When I opened up about this, my friend K told me about a book she was reading on the epidemic of loneliness. This epidemic emerges from social media use in a world where our human interactions are increasingly replaced with screen time. Another friend, H, told me that her similar feelings of loneliness and alienation in her personal life came from knowing the state of the world and witnessing the suffering of so many people around the globe. These points of disconnection flare, and I see how they affect my emotional state. It feels impossible to engage in a world where I am walking around with a broken heart.

I see the lighthouse at the highest point of the trail, its weathered red – almost rose – head burgeoning into view. Though just before I see Heceta Head's tell-tale building, I catch a sharp flash, a severe glint: it's the Fresnel lens catching the light and forcing it into the same direction rather than dispersing it. My heart, broken as it is, feels jolted alive, as if also caught by the lens, that remarkable feat of engineering.

Heceta Head is fifty-six feet tall and its lighthouse beam is visible for twenty-one miles, which makes it the Oregon coast's most powerful light. I watch for its signature intently this time, which today is a white flash every ten seconds. This flash is actually the result of a rotating lens, and though everything is electric now, once lighthouse keepers had to wind up the light like it was a grandfather clock. From my position just above the lighthouse, I watch the movement of its orbit, the lens mesmerising as it towers above the blue ocean water.

In *Stargazing,* his memoir on being a young Scottish lighthouse keeper in the 1970s, Peter Hill recounts how, in one lighthouse, the light was wound by keepers every thirty minutes. I think of what it might have been like within Heceta Head's walls as a lighthouse keeper on a different coast than Hill, but still performing the same orderly tasks. As someone who overlooked the ocean every day while enclosed from the world. I think of the question Hill's fellow keepers asked him soon after he took up his post: 'Have you started dreaming about the sea yet?'

Another tributary of my loneliness is the lack of reciprocity embedded in my artform. Perhaps this is not so different to the lighthouse that both fences itself into a space of its own, but also, at its core, exists to rescue those who might be lost at sea. Though rife with literary symbolism and meaning, *that* is ultimately its purpose, and it is not a symbiotic one. Writing poetry is inescapably a vulnerable act when it is shared with others, with strangers, and this act is placed in a narrative framework outside of my control. Sometimes it's not my handling of an image that someone finds compelling; they want my life story and my true experiences to move them. And we are, as authors, now more than ever, presented next to our work. We give so much of ourselves both through the lyricism itself and our lives that exist peripherally to it.

There is something unbearably lonely about translating the most intimate parts of your life into an artform which is then to be consumed – and to do this knowing there will be a lack of reciprocity on the other end. And I think poetry, with its often semi-autobiographical angles and unique position relative to subjectivity, is especially susceptible to this specific kind of consumption.

I begin the descent to the lighthouse, down switchbacks and occasionally a set of stairs, and admire Heceta Head's beauty. It's the most photographed lighthouse on the Oregon coast, a work of art turned into numerous images that are shared and consumed as well. I am so glad to be here, to see its contours and shapes from different angles. To feel a sense of safe return onto the shores of this place that I once called home. But part of me knows I am also extracting something from the scene, using the lighthouse and the forested world that surrounds it to find feelings of peace. To romanticise my existentialism.

In *The Loneliness Files*, the essayist Athena Dixon says that her loneliness 'is not groundbreaking' and later asks the question, 'What is the legacy we each leave behind if not some lingering performance of how we lived?' Loneliness is an emotional landscape that accumulates in those moments when we are rotated or turned away. Without realising, very slowly, it begins to take on its blurred shape – one that is both difficult to pin down and yet, somehow, everywhere. I've spoken with enough friends who are floating in this same difficult space to know that my loneliness, like Dixon's, is not groundbreaking. But neither am I sure when it really started, or when the act of poetry took on more performance than truth.

At Heceta Head Lighthouse, with both ocean and forest in my viewfinder, I think to myself that I would like to find a middle ground. I promise myself to find a shoreline – or shorelines; meeting places where my genuine self and my art can co-exist without one towering over the other.

52.8733° N, 118.0823° W

In no particular order, a sequence of memories before the disorder

; I thought of the morning we woke up together inside a deep green tent, its nylon flysheet the same colour as a Jasper wood in summer. Around us, the elk stirred and plodded and pulled at leaves. I didn't want to emerge from the zip entrance and into real life. I could hear their brassy calls and see the elusive outlines of their giant bodies. I was suspended in a dream with you. We listened to Cervidae jazz and felt contentment. I let myself have that.

; The water cupped in my hands is a fragment of the sea. The water cupped in my hands is a fragment of his story. The water cupped in my hands is translucent shame and I can almost ignore it. The water cupped in my hands is a migrant revision. The water cupped in my hands is passed on to another pair of hands and just look at all the leakage.

; In Mallorca, we were out hiking on the shortest day of the winter. Before sunrise, I woke up and dressed in all my gear. The early climb was steep and exhausting and I did it to prove to myself that I could. I remember thinking that the torrential rain and the darkness came unexpectedly. The rocks below us were sharp and wet and I couldn't see them. We walked cliffside for hours. The village lighthouse oozed in the distance. At regular intervals, its beacon of light entered my vision. This went on for the duration of my panic attack.

; I am the selfish sister. I am the selfish sister. I am the selfish sister. I am the selfish sister that hides in the refrain. I am the selfish sister that makes poetry out of pain.

; In the therapist's office after a friend's death, I was taken aback when asked if I was angry. I remember the doctor's face as he said it, his striking glasses, his shaggy grey hair. The session was free because I grieved hard enough and someone noticed. I didn't meet with him again. In retrospect, I wasn't angry at all. Still, I didn't do anything right. I don't wonder anymore why I never healed.

; This paragraph is written amidst the urge to vomit. This has been my body for decades and I still don't understand how it works. Forgive me, but I still don't love it at all.

; On the northern coast of Zanzibar, we donned our swimsuits and ran into the sea. He was still there, somewhere on the island, and the sound of his singing mixed with the roar of the waves. That year, I documented everything. There are voice clips and photos on my hard drive, but they hurt too much to look at. One night we sat outdoors with the man who later stole from him. There was a language barrier and, for a time, my self-centred concerns about first tongues obscured the greater devastations of our immigration. Instead of speaking, we watched bats flicker through tropical and unfamiliar trees. I realised I was a guest there. I was a tourist.

; To black out a bad memory is a survival technique. To black out a bad memory is a gift I've given myself so as to not lose my capacity for love.

; When I wire-transferred the money, I did it to make myself feel better for the abandonment. I was in Banff at the time and I had just walked the Bow Falls Trail. I was seeking an epiphanic moment. The sky was lavender, as so often, and the national park was uncharacteristically quiet. I wanted to come away from the riverside walk with a story to tell. I wanted to obscure the truth of my tendency to run away with precisely crafted tenderness. Because I was given a studio with a writer's desk, I thought I should dress the world up in the beauty of a lyric poem. I wrote the lines with my phone notifications on mute. I don't bother asking why the cost of a visa is so high anymore, or why their application was denied. My apathy is a marker of my citizenship. The world is so ugly and it makes me so ugly.

; Once, I came out of the ocean and admitted the truth. The significance of my body in a body of water is only a myth. That morning, I did it for the awe of the onlooker. I wanted to be someone who felt solace in nature and stomached the cold when no one else could. I wanted validation more than I wanted comfort.

; At the book launch, I dedicated a poem to him and talked about the Atlantic Ocean in my work. The Atlantic is the sight of so much violence, and this is a violence that is ongoing. It is also a marker of my diaspora. Even at that moment, it was the ocean water that separated us. I think of that night as forked time, as two alternate realities. I glanced at the livestream with each alhamdulillah. Meanwhile, fourteen thousand kilometres away, he was taken to the hospital in a state of what resembled psychosis. I didn't know until the next day. The precursor to my pain is recorded somewhere. The iteration lives on.

; When he said he no longer believed in Allah, I could no longer ignore the shadow at the edge of our lives. I don't want to tell this story. All I can say is nothing is ever new and everything is only ever revealed.

; I remember the short walk from the bus stop to our townhouse in Millwoods. I traced that path almost every day for six years. In winter, it was dark by late afternoon. In the darkness, I walked past a man-made lake while listening to Lykke Li. It shone illustriously under the neighbourhood lights and I took a detour across the bridge over the water. What is a home supposed to look like? Can an artificial lake hold the depths of true childhood? I had to pass the 7-Eleven that he worked at for less than a month, quitting soon after the shop was held up at gunpoint. When he still lived there, the front room smelled like agarbatti and canola oil.

; On the anonymous online forum, a user says that without the medication, they wouldn't be here. Below that, there is another post titled *why do we hate taking our meds?* Every week, on his way to buy milk from the drugstore, he would stop to feed the birds. I used to think differently, but now I know that tossing stale bread onto the verge is not a cure.

; I flip to the middle of the novel and read it in fragments. Linearity seems like a concept that only emerges in writing workshop critiques. I wonder how he experiences time. I read a sentence about brain damage that scares me.

; Bhanu Kapil asks, 'Do psychiatrists register the complex and rich vibrations produced by their dreaming subjects?' I remember the time he saw a figure with bright red hair circumventing his hospital bed. He was in a dreamlike state, having just awoken from an induced coma. I remember as a child, a recurring nightmare I had of being chased through labyrinthine tunnels by someone unknown. I remember it as a wholly black and white dream except for the colour bright red. The image of this stranger plagues us.

; A home is any place, any geographical or temporal location, haunted by familiar ghosts.

; For a long time, it was a poorly hidden secret. I only had to look. Instead, I spent a lifetime averting my eyes. Now, I can trace back every symptom. Where does an illness originate? All this time, I wanted to make my migrant story digestible. I hiked in Kananaskis and translated my footfall onto the page. As if the foothills could heal me and I could climb my way over the schism forced apart by my brown skin. I triangulated language, self and landscape until the lines blurred between experience and aesthetic.

; In Victoria Park in London, I sprawled across a picnic blanket and marvelled at the warm air. I felt the rural plains of Alberta dissipate from my memory. The flat landscape was a privilege I never valued. I kept my rental bike propped against a tree. I owned so few belongings. He had been here before I was born and, unlike me, he never chose this country for himself. From that, I knew this place was not my home.

; I feel safe in the grief of displacement. I read about the colonial history that marked my family's lives and it stirs righteousness in me. Within this kind of pain, even in my personal sadness, I never have to face myself. The grief of leaving also orbits around a distance. But this grief is a mirror. In it, I catch sight of myself. I catch sight of the failed daughter.

; Twice in my life, language has truly terrified me. Once, you called the ambulance because I couldn't remember your name. I couldn't speak and so I screamed. Once, I was told over the phone that, somehow, suddenly, he could no longer remember English or anyone's face. It was neurological and it was a product of migration. He could only speak his mother tongue.

; At a viewpoint on the cliffs above the Oregon coast, I stared directly at the sun as it set. I knew that I shouldn't, but I didn't want to miss the moment the bright globe disappeared beneath the horizon. I thought, what was the point of being there if I couldn't look. When I turned to you again, you were marred with pink spots, imprinted by the moment. I let myself have that too.

; Some mornings, I wake up and I feel it. The burden of inheritance.

; The elk had tags on their ears. They weren't wild. We put the tent up on a patch of land cleared specifically for our enjoyment. The hinges of our camping stove creaked and displaced the sound of their grazing. Through the car window, we could see the next campsite over. It was also awash with large animals and their shining brown hides. Before the disorder, the future was endless possibility. I didn't know then that I was a doll in a dollhouse.

6.8165° S, 39.2894° E

The Permeable Archive

After *The Vertical Interrogation of Strangers* by Bhanu Kapil

Who are you and whom do you love?

My mother visits Scotland for the first time. She travels the long distance from Edmonton to Edinburgh in the heat of July. I have been here for over seven years, and this is the first time she will see the ecology that my body is slowly shaping itself around: the slant of the Scottish gales, the heads of its thistles, the spines of its ribboning, rocky Munros. When she arrives, I'm surprised to learn that she feels the same tidal pull toward the water that I do. Somehow, I didn't know this about her. But now I understand that this is my inheritance: the glazed moon and the tides that must have first lived in her before in me. The lightness. The buoyancy. The gasp that follows that first ice-cold sip of water – all of it passed down. There is her black swimsuit and mine, both caught on film from the back, and the two of us later peering into the photo, appreciating the contours of our skins. The eastern coast brings forward undulating waves that mark us; they reveal how I am an iteration of my mother in this way I'm only just now discovering. This new understanding unfolds like an extended scroll of history. Here, in this place I once felt so lonely, the sea translates our figures into itemised echoes of love. I am her, drawn slightly differently in the present tense. We are repetitions of the silvery coastal water that designs the sand into coalescent ripples. I look in the mirror. I look at the reflection of her face with every glance in every single body of water. When she returns home, I still look for her in the depths. The sea is another reminder of displacement.

*

Where did you come from / how did you arrive?

It has blurred edges. Dar es Salaam in my memory. I did my best to archive what I could. My notes are written by a past self who sifted through sensations of sweat and salt. Ultimately, it was that other self that decided what was important enough to keep. Would I choose the same things now? How else would I capture the landscape, the dark nights with their swooping bats, the churning machinery of the sea? I thought so much about first lost languages back then, so much about the adhan, so much about *origins*. I think now of geography, of conservation, of justice, of the skin memories lost to water and to time. Where the city's shoreline dips inward, into an estuary of the Indian Ocean, there are wetlands and mangrove wetlands. These blend into what become wooded areas or grasslands and low shrubs. Eventually, they entangle with the dark green boreal forests of my childhood. She is archiving too, always, my young self. Much of what I know is summarised in the blur outside a car window or an online leaflet about the pressures on Dar es Salaam's green spaces. An imagined place, I realise, only comes into existence when it is given a story. I peer into the myth that made me. To circumvent a mirage is at the heart of artmaking. In all that I write, there is the figurative homeland and the figuration of a girl. I walk around in the symbol of home, its long grasses and red clay roads making space for new and invented meaning. In *From From*, Monica Youn writes that 'revealing a racial marker in a poem is like revealing a gun in a story or like revealing a nipple in a dance. After such a revelation, the poem is *about* race, the story is *about* the gun, the dance is *about* the body of the dancer – it is no longer considered a dance at all and is subject to regulation.' In the past, I was so distraught about the perceived otherness of my body and obsessed with my own rootlessness. It reached the point where I turned my ego into an imagined country. In *The Antilles: Fragments of Epic Memory*, Derek Walcott writes, 'History can alter the eye and the moving hand to conform a view of itself; it can rename places for the nostalgia in an echo; it can temper the glare of tropical light to elegiac monotony in prose, the tone of judgement in Conrad, in the travel journals of Trollope.' I am relearning. I am working against History, with a capital H – the rigid archive and all it overwrites in its colonial sweep.

*

How will you begin?

In *Dear Memory*, Victoria Chang asks, 'What happens when memory's place of origin disappears?' I tell myself that it's okay that I have changed, that the person I used to be is nowhere to be found. I let myself mourn her. Eventually, I detach from my body and become a floating mind, feeling deeply displaced from poetry, my chosen medium of artmaking. I look elsewhere, anywhere else, besides the ongoing turmoil of the page. When I begin attending life-drawing sessions, I feel connected to the body in a new and invigorating way. Not only my body, the body I am trying to relearn and love better, but to *bodies* in general. Every session is an experiment. In that room in central Edinburgh, coincidentally called the 'Anatomy Room', a new respite evolves. I feel free to test out the curves of different figures and I attempt to shade them in. From these careful tasks, I begin to notice the tiny movements and gestures that I would have otherwise never paid attention to. Not even in my poetry did I ever grasp, understand, attend to, or think about *light* in so many enamouring ways as I do in these two-hour sessions. The tactility of using pencil to trace the ambiguity of light onto the page is provocative. I revel in the movements of one body as it changes another body – a drawn body – according to pressure and space: the tender arc of my wrist, the gentle or hard pressing down of graphite onto the page, and the resulting thickness of a line. A figure emerges onto the shore of my sketchbook, tumbling forward from my own amateur hand like a nascent wave. It is as if this movement itself, the drag of a simple pencil, is an origin story. In its grazing, what it draws mimics the way we enter the world: imprinted by the ghosts of the ancestors, the mirror images that make us; I watch the body become. I watch its double change position. It is easy to forget, sometimes, in the written word, how profound it is to make something. How much it matters to invite art into the world and nourish it into being. I urge myself to begin.

*

How will you live now?

The problem with looking back is that all my preferred landscapes are dreams. I try to embed love here, at the intersection between *a childhood memory of small-town northern Alberta* and a public footpath in the Scottish Highlands, where I'm walking alongside a tributary far from its source. I steep my hiking boots in mud that coagulates in their rubber grooves. I'm on a river path that seems to lead away from my family, away from the Midwestern prairies where I was born. That specific composition of mud. The source of my own tributaries. There is no end in sight. I try to embed love here, at the glaciated remains of my inheritance. The ongoing melt of my personal history is an entanglement of heritage that, as a child riven with colonial learnings, I did not bother to value. I wanted, instead, the pathway to elsewhere. A landscape where assimilation led to areas of decay. I try to embed love here, still, knowing it isn't too late to live purposefully, with the knowledge of my ancestors, the woman who crossed one river after another river. So, I turn toward saplings growing in the fissures cracked open by time. I transport them, gently, to my homeland – any place with birch trees. They are soaking wet in the ongoing rain. Damp leaves reflect my earliest dreams. Whatever buds here is a symbol of renewal and regeneration, a reminder of the elliptical world, the way love cycles back into the body: what is lost isn't lost. New growth comes from past memories.

*

What is the shape of your body?

Sometimes when I write poetry, it feels like I am leaking from the seams of my body. In this act of creation there is that fluid moment before anything is really shaped or refined. Instead, something unruly and electric spills out onto the page, filling a previously blank space with messy tendrils of art that demands to be expressed. I realise that, in my poetry, I am always trying to articulate the shape of my body. I've noticed there are words that I use again and again, words that stand in for the way I embody multiplicity, threading together narratives propelled by echoes. 'Dark' is an obvious one – dark hair, dark skin, *too dark, too dark, too dark*. There are also the words 'chasm' and 'sieve' and 'water'. And then, there is what is perhaps my favourite, a word that has appeared here already: 'tendril'. Yes, I think the shape of my body is a tendril. When I encounter 'tendril' for the first time – in the beginning – I visualise the climbing plant, its threadlike appendage, its spiralling form. I visualise a sliver of green that burgeons from language, somehow lengthening a poetic line because we imagine its lengthening body. I notice its shape. It can also refer to something that resembles a plant tendril, like a ringlet of hair. I think of my hair when I emerge from different waters, wet with different ghosts. The word tendril has a softness in how it moves. I think something is pulled from me, perhaps a memory or an indescribable emotion, when I say it. Within the expanse of this word is my whole body, unsure of itself as it crosses borders. It stretches and uncurls, it spirals, it contracts, it climbs into new spaces. It does not replace one space for another. It does not leave. Rather, it is a node, an ongoing point of connection, a long, outstretched hyphen.

*

What do you remember about the earth?

I have been invited to travel north across the Scottish landscape for a writing residency at Moniack Mhor, a place where I have felt my heart and body relax in ways I can rarely replicate. To get to the converted croft and its staggering views of Glen Strathfarrar and Ben Wyvis, I first travel by train up through the Scottish mountains. They are still caught in that magical moment when the hillsides are overcome with heather. The train's path toward Inverness takes a route up the west side of the Cairngorms, a mountain range with some of the country's highest summits. These mountains have their own myriad of tales and are beloved by the nature writer Nan Shepherd, for whom, in a world both disturbed and uncertain, they were her 'secret place of ease'. Between the braiding carpet of lush green and purple, I watch as we pass by forests, too, at a speed that offers too short a glimpse. I keep my eye trained on the world as it quickens outside my window, and I do so with an eagerness reserved for the north, the risen latitude that always draws me in. There's a knowingness in my body when I move in its direction; a sense of peace; of home, no matter where in the world I am. In Scotland's ancient Caledonian forests there are pine remnants that have adapted to the wet and windy climate. These remains are tethered to nine thousand years of ecological history. The forests' handsome trees remind me of the lodgepole pine commonly found in areas very near to where I grew up in Alberta. Over time, the images of both types of pine have seeped steadily into my poetry, their grizzly edges always darkly tinged or festooned with cold weather in memory. As the lush green reality of the earth and its long archive unfurl, I begin to feel a familiar anxiety over my own liminality, the way I sometimes find myself feeling unclasped by the world, as if not concretely from any place at all. This anxiety troubles me, even if for the most part, I think, *what does it matter?* What does it matter to be a suspended mind, laterally reaching outward and constantly walking the perimeter of impossible in-betweens? A collector of mirage, an artmaker who tries to make the mirage real.

*

What are the consequences of silence?

I have always felt drawn to a poetics of the environment, toward a kind of literature where revelation and emotion are symbolised by the natural world. In this way, my poetry is a marker of place and my connection to it – the dark cliffsides on the Oregon coast, or the streaming golden canola fields of Alberta, scattered with spotted calves. Given this impulse to write and read about nature, given how elements of nature run through my work like an infinite network of rivers, why did I, for so long, hesitate to call myself a nature writer? I wonder where this self-silencing began and why it was so pervasive. What was it about Western traditions of nature writing, of landscape poetry and of ecopoetry, that felt so outside of my reach? My relationship to nature is an embodied one, and it is also one that is intricately layered. I know, now, that carving out space in the Western context of nature writing as a woman of colour involves work – a continuous learning and unlearning, a continuous resistance against a genre that is steeped in whiteness and bias. My work exists in a context where, as stated by Sandeep Parmar, writing by racialised writers is misread as a 'direct expression of their racial otherness'. My work is, to various degrees, intertwined with all of the aforementioned traditions of ecological writing and modes of ecological thought. My body and my art ravel against the gatekeeper that shuts out my voice. In her essay 'To That Silence, I Told Everything', Xiao Yue Shan writes, 'how powerful silence is, one realises, when one knows what detonates and riles and resounds directly beneath it'. I no longer shy away from the words beneath that silence, but I interrogate the places where they roil.

*

Tell me what you know about dismemberment.

I visit the Aburi Botanical Gardens in Ghana, West Africa, and of course it feels immediately soothing to emerge onto a walkway lined with beautiful royal palm trees. This is especially true after inching forward in Accra's traffic, in a heat I'm not used to, all the way toward the Akwapim-Togo Ranges. While in the gardens, I marvel at the huge elliptical and vibrantly green calabash fruit that is so heavy it pulls the plant's branches down closer to the earth. I feel genuinely delighted in my smallness next to impossibly large monstera leaves. However, despite its current role in bio conservation and modern agriculture, the history of the gardens is one rooted in the ownership of land by an oppressor. Here, 6.8 hectares of earth were cleared and cultivated in this mountainous region during the British colonial era, and British curators implanted species from South and Southeast Asia in the gardens, as well as from many other places. A plaque at the gardens' entrance lists its curators and botanists, and the names are distinctly, historically British. They are time-stamped from an era of imperialism. The gardens were cultivated as a place for colonial officers to be comfortable, their location in the Akwapim-Togo Mountains selected to allow them to recuperate, like I was now, from the heat. I read that word, 'recuperate', and in this context, its four syllables have never made me recoil more. The information makes me wonder who the *nature cure*, a phrase that feels increasingly like a particular kind of branding, was ever for. This is a question that reverberates into the present day. In touring the gardens with my friend S as a guide, I feel both unease and peace. These emotions bloom in me when I think of the clearings, cultivation, and the history of theft that is so invisible on the map I looked at to get here. It was nowhere between the animated greens and blues. What is a written map if not a scholarly tool of omission? I look at the map fitted on the device in my palm and all I see is colonial iconography that designs an artificial image of the earth. This is an earth that is bisected by borders and variegated hues. Regions all over the world were partitioned despite the land memories across them. The written map is a political map that erases the route of transgenerational spirits across arbitrary and often violent borders: between one country and another, between a city and its once inaccessible green spaces. At the gardens, my new knowledge meets sweating bodily tissue and rounded calabash curve. How much violence lives in the schism between arrive and archive?

*

Describe a morning you woke without fear.

I read *Fourth Person Singular* by Nuar Alsadir in three spaces across different days in the Scottish Highlands: very early in the morning at the desk in my bedroom; sprawled on a blanket outside, overlooking the infinitely textured hills; and in the common room next to the fire. It's a slim volume, something I expected to finish in a single sitting, in a single room. But the pages contain poetry interspersed with lyric essays and other prose-like sections that resist categorisation. It is a smart and difficult book. I think I will need to reread it and read around it, submerging myself in its theoretical concepts. I'm already attached to it. The book is like a forest where you encounter several paths, choosing one, for now, with the intention of returning to take the others. While here in the Highlands, I wake up in the mornings and go for a run around the nearby paths. The cattle watch me as I pass by, my heart thumping with the blood and exhaustion of exercise but otherwise threaded with a quiet joy. When I return, I place my books in a stack underneath the windowsill. Though I have read a lot at the desk in my room, I have written very little. The writing process has its own hills and valleys, its shards of pine tree, its patchwork farmlands. I look outside my window at the unending layers of green surrounding the croft. The landscape feels like an apt metaphor for what it's like to be a poet sometimes. Steep inclines, jagged descents, rough bogland, and miles and miles of vibrant, rolling grassland. At the end of a long project, it can be difficult to imagine a new world of poems, a new manuscript, a new plot of land. Right now, prose is slipping through me and onto the page: messy, unadorned, meandering, ready to be shaped. I render the fog and its uncertain opacity. I piece apart its qualities in a drawn-out breath. This feels new and hard. But that fricative challenge is, itself, precious. The difficulty of not knowing something and needing to learn it is important and meaningful. The morning palpitates like a fiercely working heart with painstaking, gorgeous creativity.

*

How will you / have you prepare(d) for your death?

I know the beginning and the end. The rest is smoke, its tendrils weaving into an enormous field of blank space. Many faces vanish into the dark night of the past. I rest underneath a sequence of memories that fade away like the inky text on a grocery receipt. I don't like to let things disappear, but they still do despite my concern, and they always will – gone like that story I once heard about Prophet Muhammad, the story that darts into the wood of my childhood like a deer slippery with rainfall. Or the one that mingles with the chapter of my father bent over his tasbih while, outside, trees snap back in the northerly wind. All that in-between space. All that cigarette smoke that clouds the memories of my small-town past. For many years now, amongst the clutches of illnesses in my family, I have lived in anticipatory grief. It drapes over everything, every emotion, every desire, obscuring the narratives underneath. The notion of death presses quietly against us. My mother tells me that I was born with a burial plot, a little section of earth, a halved and halved again slot of prairie. I wonder if it is next to my grandfather's plot in Calgary, those fragments of his life that I've always wondered about. My sisters have one too. All of us do, in the vicinity of one another. This is a tradition, or even a methodology, to keep us together beyond the materiality of our bodies. This is a metaphysical kind of togetherness. I was born into a religion that wants to eternally house my soul. My mother tells me about my burial plot when I'm visiting home, luggage thrown in the back seat, the oceanic distance sweetly closed between us. We have spent our lives wandering away from one another only to arrive together, again, someday in death. Later, my mother sits next to me with our whippet, Samantha, stretched out between us and the bright winter sun streaming in through wide windows. The light strikes our hands in a way that suggests forever. The whole visit I think about past lives and what might have come before the beginning.

I think of all the life I will tread across and all the land that I will eventually become. Deer. Soil. Daughter. Wind. Smoke. Rain. Amen.

*

And what would you say if you could?

It's not enough. Grief enters the dream body and something inside shifts. The lens through which I view the world is one of constant change. All things, even the mundane, slot into before and after. I picture a hard, round knot inside my chest. Something in-between the size of a glass bead and a marble. Every so often, I think it rolls or slides and I feel a twinge. Other times, it's a large object, both invasive and flaring, too great to tamp down, too nebulous to unwind. These days, everything feels like a raw nerve. I see a small bird enclaved in a small tree and call it grief. At the height of the worst storm of the year, I fixate on roadside ferns splitting wildly in the red warning wind. My floral duvet is peeled apart and I refuse to leave my bed. Is it okay to put that here, in this visible and public space? This is an admission of my flaws and sorrows. I wonder if it's my trespass as the author of these words, or the trespass of the person who reads them. Poetry itself rarely feels like *enough*, not nearly as often as it feels like spectacle. Another shift. Grief is the cold weather grazing. Grief is the dim lamplight growing darker. Grief is the missed video call or else its grainy picture. Grief is the dullest pull at the most sensitive heart. Grief is listening to 'Blue Is the Eye' while driving further away from home. Grief is green hills and farmland and first lost languages in the distance. Grief is the inability to describe the always cooling tea. Grief is the artist on stage whose eyes close as they hit the perfect note and suddenly you think *oh my god why am I crying?*

Water

28.3587° N, 14.0537° W

An ocean lyric

At the ocean, I find myself writing again after a months-long pause, but the writing feels amorphous, shapeless. Pages and pages about the sea as a metaphor. It feels like my words are too earnest, the very truth of my mind on the page, but also meaningless, going nowhere. Is metaphor enough? Is the lyric mode enough?

My notebook fills with observations about the water and the waves, each fragment ending at the shoreline of my memory.

A brilliant gradient of turquoise. Fuerteventura is cupped by the Northern Atlantic Ocean; it is salty and glittering. I go in naked and my body feels sleek, weightless – I think I know then something about the way the seals in Orkney must feel, gliding effortlessly through the cool water. Droplets of the sea collect all along the ridge of my back. To swim like this fills me with energy, a current sweeping through my body, a kind of shockwave that I thought had been forever displaced, submerged in different shades of grief. To swim here, with the person I love, the water so clear and so accepting, is captivating.

It is early November and there is a heatwave. I am in up to my waist, the ocean lapping its way up my darkened skin. I shiver with each climbing ripple. In that moment, I am strangely both extremely aware of and, for once, completely dispassionate about the exact contours of my body. I hope I can retrieve this sensation in the future. This indifferent attitude toward what my body looks like. All my attention focused solely on how it feels. Gorgeous, that Sunday, so gorgeous as I slip into the water fully at last.

We look out at the horizon, and he says through a grin, you can see ocean for miles. It's all you can see. It's true. All that brilliant, unbelievable blue.

I often talk about water being a place of crossings and connections, of separation and togetherness. Today, the water leaps away from coherence, from comprehensible thought. It is an immersive pool, a thing of awe. The ocean feels bigger than my language.

At Playa de Sotavento de Jandía, I watch the waves crash onto the shore. Then I think 'crash' isn't the right word because of the way its syllable is harsh in the mouth. The waves move slowly, languidly, onto the shore, taking their time. They are gentle. At the horizon, the Atlantic looks still, calm, unmoving. It goes on and on that way, mystery lurking beneath its vivid face.

It isn't until they are near the shore that the swell of the waves becomes visible to my eye. It's a slow, extended journey across the scope of saltwater. I feel like that sometimes. I feel like I've travelled a long distance, quietly, imperceptibly, across the vastness of a clear, turquoise, resplendent ocean, with all my peaks and troughs and traumas invisible to the eye, lingering in the depths of ancestral history. It is such a long, such an imperceptible journey, that the particularities of any series of waves are lost.

In the oceanic archives, hidden from even the most curious of descendants, there is the northern border of India riddled with monsoon weather and vibrating tectonic plates. There are water crossings assisting the centuries-long conversions to Islam across the world. In Northern Gujarat, there is the unworkable land with its precious, rare, desalinated rain.

At the site of erosion, there is the religious persecution that wetted skin with violence. Generations later, there is that different ocean that doubled as a portal, a threshold I myself keep crossing only to never arrive.

Water is an object the same strange way skin is an organ: uncontained, reaching, seamless. The calm here surprises me. When the movement begins, when the object, silky smooth water, starts to make a sound (a sound like an entire boreal forest shivering in the wind), it does so in such a small, inobtrusive way. All that it has inherited, its protracted, looming self that is made of centuries of saltwater, stays hidden in the depths.

Nothing but a tiny crest breaking onto the shore to suggest that I have migrated at all.

//

It's midday in the first week of November. Today we are on a different shoreline, on Playa del Moro. My notebook is splayed open in the wind, sand collecting on its pages. I don't know how to articulate the scene with words, not in English, not in the sparse knowledge of my first lost language and its mystifying origin either. But in my head, I see the whole glorious image. My mind holds in it the entire Atlantic Ocean and my small body within the waves.

Start with a brown body, a relatively tiny smudge against the sand dunes. Bare feet sinking deep into the mound, the surrounding land carved out exactly this way, this perfect way, over eons. It isn't about the size of a body of a woman relative to a body of water anymore. There is also the size, stretching, wide and hungry, of time itself.

I move forward until I'm standing in the blue-green water. Almost instantly, and without the usual slow crawl up my feet——calves——hips——waist——stomach, my legs lift up off the part-sandy, part-rocky seabed. I'm surprised to be afloat so soon, forced in deep by the power of the water.

To stare straight ahead and see giant, riveting, glorious waves coming toward you. This is the feeling I can't explain. I don't want to love the ocean and its intimidation, but I do. A love that sits deep in my chest and is, I think, partly born out of very plain fear.

The sound of their crash onto the shore reverberates in the air. This time, it is undoubtedly a crash, and it is commanding. I wonder how the sound of water here can be so different from elsewhere. Then I think perhaps it is not the water, but the woman within it. That when confronted with the truth of the sea, I latch onto my terror and, like a camera filter, it alters the image. The noise is somewhere behind me, too far behind me, I think. It raises the hair at the back of my neck.

The waves: fearless, tumultuous, careening of their own furious volition, heading straight for my sun-washed silhouette as I float numbly in the vast, glittering, fathomless sea.

That feeling of being so small, in fact, so meaningless, in a heaving space.

In a heaving space between the oncoming wave and its collapse on my skin. In a heaving space where my mind goes from racing, anxious, loud, prickling to almost totally silent. I become a blank channel of static in the face of something so much larger, so much more significant, than any one of my sadnesses.

Or perhaps not sadness. According to the therapist, who I have since stopped seeing, it is anger. My own lack of control, or perhaps even the reality of not doing enough. The subtext of sadness, the marginal notes of sorrow, the sharp crack of a breaking heart, the pain that is iced out by the cold ocean water, the rawness of my body pricked with sand and salt – all of this is a glaze attempting to conceal the ceramic hardness of my self-loathing.

In the face of so much undulating, terrifying blue, I am dispersed.

I notice that heaving space. I attend to it. The oncoming wave, its grazing and its swishing, moves toward the sand dunes on the shore. At the last second, the quiet, my blank, unknowing mind, fills at once like a well with anticipation. I acknowledge my inability, no matter what I do, no matter my strength, to stop the layer of rising seawater from finding my body. It will, perhaps, cover me totally in its salt. It will, perhaps, even carry me away from myself.

In Playa del Moro, I hear those same waves continuing past my sunken, wet shoulders. Their pattern goes on behind me, thrashing along a short journey before unravelling, as if exhausted, into the shallows.

Just moments ago, I was in the fierce seawater, my body buoyant and gleeful in the waves, trembling at the awe of their clear, magnificent movements. On my way out, I had struggled to get free from their depths and back onto the sand, to become that smudge on dry land once more. The waves were so large, the crests of them moving more quickly than I had anticipated.

Next to me, on a damp towel, he says it's unusual to feel the wind on your whole body. I realise, despite the generations of heat that made me, I now make my home in cold climates. We lie there, sand gathering on our still wet skin. We are post-swim, post-fear of the waves, with the sun angled down right at us, and the wind – everywhere.

When I was in the water, watching the sea peel straightforwardly toward me, I knew I wanted to capture something of the waves' absolute verticality, the way they seemed to carry a deeper, darker, more troubled blue within them, peaks eventually quivering onto greener water and mixing their sorrows together. I also knew that I had assigned myself an impossible task. How could anyone ever accurately describe the visual of those hues mingling, or the feeling of overwhelm that follows?

The sun feels so hot and the colour of the world is bright underneath it. Yet, somehow, still, in the distant water, where the coils of spray had picked up my body and deposited it wherever they may have wished, the same sky looks wilder, cloudy. Menacing, actually, as if when I was there, in the turbulent water, I was in the midst of a concentrated storm.

//

Today's swim was early, on a different land mass. Yesterday, after our swim at Playa del Moro, we hung over the rails of the ferry, watching the Spanish island we'd departed become smaller and smaller, its clarifying edges blurring with distance. We were moving to another island, one further north that creased the Atlantic with its different shape.

I look at a photo of me leaning against the vessel, hair whipping around my face, a smile visible through dark, untameable strands. This is my figure caught in a moment of brazen joy. I feel guilt, transported into a reality that the metaphor of water and its solemnity, its veneration, cannot touch. I will remember my time here forever. This moment of disappearing from the world, unreachable, with no data, no scrolling. I feel guilty for my stopgapped grief.

My peace of mind is a product. It is manufactured and feels wrong, like the plastic bottles adorning the streets, droplets of potable water clinging to their ridged edges.

When we disembarked the ferry, we made our way to the marina where the unmoving boat we were to sleep on was tethered. It swayed as we clambered on, sand clinging to our unwashed bodies, not yet having visited the public showers a short distance away from the pier. We sat on the deck and ate toast, our conversation punctuated by fish jumping out of the still seawater, their splashes cutting clear through the silence of docked and empty boats and the lack of waves.

My phone picked up signal and flashed with a whirl of notifications. Trump had that day won the election in the US and everything I saw was saturated with mourning. The mourning runs deeper than one government over the other. It is an entire nation, a world, engulfed in the loss of trust, the loss of faith, in a network of political systems that value capital over life, that cannot denounce genocide. It is a betrayal. It is a recognition of the work ahead, the dismantling of a society and its deeply corrupt framework.

I read a poem by Lena Khalaf Tuffaha titled 'what to the Arab American is election day'. Election day is, she writes, 'a Tuesday in the second November of the Genocide.' A friend from America, now living in Edinburgh, said they wished they could do more, be on the ground. I felt the slats over my eyes waver, rippling away like elliptical water after the quickness of jumping fish.

A decade ago, I had studied writing in Oregon and I often reminisce of my time there with fondness. A few years later, in the autumn of 2016, close to the deadline for grad school applications, Trump was elected for the first time. The thought of immigrating to America again as a brown, Muslim, queer woman within that context had filled me with unassailable fear. I might have been there, otherwise, on the ground. Instead, I am now an onlooker, a lucky voyeur offering solidarity, offering my tears, and feeling the shame of futility.

I shrink into myself, as if making the body take up less space can change the body's impact. As if I can hide the ways I am complicit.

//

The shoreline is a stretch of sand between black rocks, their gleaming sharp boundaries leaning in like two laden arms. The beach is flanked by these dark cliffs, and there is a seemingly inert, watery space between. A held space, where the waves are calmer than those that struck me the other day, that dislodged my secret terror. This morning, when I step into the water, I don't see the sky darken portentously, and the rhythm of the sea doesn't absorb my trembling. There are small undulations clamouring over the ocean to meet my inconsequential body, a gentle lapping at my feet.

Here, between the cliffs, nestled on a stretch of sand clear of the rough and jagged rocks, I feel obscenely safe.

I come back to love. A love for swimming and being in the water. I remember Sylvan Lake as a child. I remember the Pacific Ocean as a young woman, so long ago now that this version also feels like, in some ways, a child. I know increasingly, with age or perhaps with the newer courage to step out further into the depths, I find myself afraid. I walk into the water at the behest of wet sand, plunging my toes deep. I eye the endless ocean ahead and feel timid as I stare outward, even where the water is shallow for a long time.

The terror comes because the ocean looks and feels and *is* vast, like a continuous and unsolvable mystery. The depth feels inconsequential. My fear is tethered instead to magnitude.

The sheer size of it, the ocean, and I revere it like I might Allah.

A few minutes into the swim, even when confronted with my own smallness, seeing the horizon held between reaching arms, knowing that powerful endless current, I feel strangely safe somehow. The waves are almost round, and I want to call them soft, with gentle curves. They are bubbling up vivaciously and I think again of small children. Of Sylvan Lake. Of letting myself inhabit that young girl again, for whom safety was a given even though safety wasn't her truth. The girl who did not know of risk and violence in such terms.

Bubbling up, like a summer reprieve just an hour south of the city I was born in. Bubbling up and floating on the surface.

The waves were not sharp. They were not crashing. I come back to love.

The sound of waves rippling onto the shore and the ocean piling onto the sand like layers of soft-serve. Then pulled back. The rhythm is exact, the pattern almost traceable before it is unexpectedly ruptured, like a masterful poem.

I submerge my body and it, seemingly at once, mixes and merges with the Atlantic waters. I swim out eagerly, my body heading straight toward the blissful horizon. But the soft waves pull me back, and I almost convince myself they do so protectively, as if we are connected, as if there is a lineage there. At one point, I kick my legs and splay my arms in front of me, desiring to go beyond, to break through the boundary of the shallows and exit the sheltering. I make some progress, my feet hovering over the sandy seabed, but for the most part I remain unmoving, unable to steer forward, my velocity stunted by the veil of the ocean. I will not cross this threshold.

Held in place. The forces guiding me forward almost equal to those holding me back.

Eventually I relent and let the water lift my legs out from underneath me. Next to the cliffs, I spread out my usually tightly coiled body. I let go of the self that is always ambitious, desperate to go forward, move ahead, do more, and I allow myself to float.

//

The next day, I'm back on Fuerteventura. The tide is coming in, and it brings with it stiff, unrelenting wind.

When we pull up to the side of the road, it is totally empty, with only us in the vicinity. Passing through the gorgeous foyer of beige-white sand dunes, we are keenly aware that we are very much alone. It is quiet, though the waves appear louder without any other witnesses. We arrive just as the sun is burgeoning, sweeping through an array of dusty white and yellow-tinted clouds. He pauses on a mound of sand, says that the sky looks very dramatic, and I look too.

Dramatic, sublime, striking, I feel there aren't any good enough words for it. When I think about Allah, and that seed of belief with its hard endocarp knotted within me, I think this is the sight, the feeling, that I am attempting to tether to faith. It is captivating, bodily affective, and I stop walking. It is unbelievable, rays streaming from the clouds as if drawing the eye to suggest that *yes*, something more, something important, something inarticulable but momentous is occurring.

The glorious threads of light are visible from the dunes but even more impressive from closer to the waterline. When the ocean's deep, hardly imaginable breadth comes into view, and the rolling and thrashing of its waves take over my senses, suddenly becoming the only thing I am able to hear, I stand in real, unfiltered awe.

The water is a slightly murkier green-blue than I have seen it before, perhaps to be called *morning ocean blue*. Where the blazing sunlight finds water, the morning ocean blue settles. It accepts the embrace and my heart twinges seriously, honestly, earnestly at this display of elemental love.

There is less wind this morning and the sound of the sea is clearer than yesterday. Louder. It amazes me how much can change on the same extended beach at different times of day, from different perspectives, at even minutely different times of year. I try to collect all the differences, like one of those games in the newspaper where you spot what's changed between two cartoon images. Part of the emotional shifting, the changed emotional relevance, is atmospheric, I know.

It is early morning and my body is cleared of sand, though already collecting stubborn beads as I write this. I am freshly washed, with soapy, alkaline skin.

The alertness of the morning, combined with my still drowsy body. And of course, the emptiness, no one but us here. These waves, their booming echoes, the exact placement of the sun from this vantage point, on this day, is ours alone. I lock it inside me, *it* being the full range of sensations and feelings, all the little things I remember or meditate on, prompted by this exact moment. Even if they are already disappearing, gone.

I've archived what I can, as fast as the ink in my pen will run, but it won't be, can't be, will never be the whole of it. All the fleeting thoughts and images.

The fragmentary imaginings of my parents growing up near an ocean with cascading waves like this one. Flickering scenes of them at the water as young people, the lifelong illness not yet debilitating, the disorder inconceivable. Unburdened, possibly healed by the salty spray, though I am not sure how much I believe in that, the nature cure, the possibly effervescent, wistful myth.

All of these images full and robust and bright in my mind, details right down to the arches of feet, the gleaming of wet eyelashes, the sediment of the 1960s, the darting fish. All of these so one-dimensional on the page compared to the vibrant, ongoing reel of film in my imagination.

But the scent, even the light, and the sheen of sweat on my physical skin. These make me think of St Lucia. Yesterday, while walking through Corralejo's main street, I thought I saw N. A young woman had her hair pulled back in a similar way, and it had the same fine texture that marked N's Swiss heritage. The woman's elegant clothes hung off her similar body shape. N, but at twenty-one or twenty-two. This past version of her smiling broadly with friends. Her ghost, her doppelgänger, also drawn to the sea.

At Gros Islet, the ocean water was surrounded not by dunes, but pitons. The riveting blue of it was salty and heavy with the island's mangoes, which she and I, and our friend A, once unpeeled and ate delightedly in the water, sweet and salty sensations reconciling in our mouths. This we did under the instruction of someone we loved and learned from, who is now gone and has been gone for close to a decade.

That water is a library keeping so many of our stories, the secrets and sometimes darknesses of our womanhood.

Its foam flourishes with our first poems, its deep inviting seawater is a memorial of our ricocheting laughter. I hear it even now, coalescing and becoming the early morning ocean blue right here, underneath the godly sun, which is no longer streaming in reverent, spiritual ways, but casting light in its usual brilliant manner.

As if Allah, as if my belief, can again retreat into my body, becoming hard, impermeable, lodged, almost uncomfortable. As if I am given permission to continue my questioning, my abstract and often vacillating faith.

When I go into the water after all my reminiscing, I am strangely already exhausted. Remembering is fraught, fallible. It requires its own kind of energy. Nostalgia embeds itself within me as it always does, makes me feel down as it always does.

It is still early, still just past nine in the morning. It looks like the tide is going out and so, I swim. Right here, and as far as I can see on either side, I am the first one in. The only one in. I recall the adage repeated and transformed by the poet Nâzım Hikmet, 'I know you can't wash in the same river even once', and that too makes me feel sad. The ephemerality and inability to return.

I am the first small dot to encounter this particular, gorgeous, enlightening cycle of the ocean's push and pull. Even on the smooth, unmarred sand, my footprints are the only neat human indents next to those of the birds.

He comes in too, his body silky behind me, holding me tenderly against his chest as the towering swells find us. A quiet happiness returns. We float in a gentle but attentive way, in the watery landscape of the present tense, our bodies lifting in small gestures then sliding back down again together.

//

The last morning. The last first morning swim. The last early sun rays breaking through the morning clouds. The last serene loneliness on the blanketing sand dunes of Playa del Moro.

I notice with astonishment how different one morning can look to another. Only twenty-four hours between them. Today, we arrive only minutes earlier than the day before, to the same sandy coast and its inviting beach. Yet, the clarity of the day, a rippling blue sky, means the sun is bright and crisp already, with no godlike clouds or moments of awe hinting toward personal religion parting through them. It's as if the universe knows the emotional tenor of a morning, and so the events of the day play out differently too.

This time, when we arrive, the beach isn't empty. Two swimmers enjoy the hot morning sun, their hair wet and blonde and shining. More trickle in, with slow ease, shades of different bodies gleaming in the stark sunlight.

I love the moment of arrival the most. I love walking toward the ocean in the first embers of daylight, my steps accumulating across the reaching, wide sand dunes.

While walking toward the shoreline, across all that sand, the quiet is, as if suddenly, replaced with the sound of the waves. To go from silent anticipation to the friction of water expanding from water sets something aflame within me. I listen to the waves pick up speed, then drop onto the shore with stimulating topples.

I pause, still some distance away from the ocean, feet dry and sinking into the patterns of sand ripples. I can hear the waves. I think I said it aloud. I can hear them.

The sound was startling in a way, despite these weeks of my body and my senses revolving around the sea. And I thought of yesterday, how instead of the ocean's sounds, I was mesmerised by the light. How I didn't quite realise, not with any exactness or acknowledgement, precisely when I crossed the cusp, the doorway, from silent dunes to furious water. My senses zeroed in on that one, glowing orb and I wonder now about all the sensations, all the exquisite, meaningful, transformative moments I've lost to this human condition. To the blur.

At half past eight, we're in, gleeful, our usual shouts about the temperature getting lost in the volume of the sea.

But the waves are tall and they refute a slow entrance. Within seconds, we are wet up to our waists, and the final swoop under is, if not easy, quick and without lingering thought or apprehension.

Deep water collects in this place, at this part of the shore. It is held where the sand winks toward the ocean, creating a bowl, or a shallow cavern. When the tide is in, the water extending across the sand and toward the dunes as far as possible, the bowl fills with water and creates deeper shallows than I'm accustomed to. I hiccup over the lip.

And I think, then say out loud, *I'm afraid*. My words are lost to the ocean.

So much has changed over so much time to sculpt the ocean. These carved and hollowed spaces have become what they are due to the resilience of water. Its fluid shape swerving between and around different living things, different terrains. What I fear, what scares me in the depth of that bowl, is this ocean, this perfect ocean, which has become and is becoming itself for so long. So much longer than my own fleeting imprint will ever be.

I emerge from the water just past noon. This will be one of my last swims at Playa del Moro, and soon I will be returning home to Scotland's cold weather and colder seas. I think of how I slipped so easily into the water that first day, my skin streamlined like an aquatic animal, unencumbered. On the east coast of Scotland, I don't normally swim at this time of year. I think of dressing my skin in my swimsuit, the one with sleeves, and entering the chilly water.

For now, the Atlantic still coats my body, a layer too, in a way. It feels like momentary freedom. I lick my lips and taste it.

There won't be the chance to wash my hair before we leave in a few hours. I think of all the sand in it, turning the usually silky, straight strands into a coarser, rougher texture. Soon, this version of me, this oceanic, salt-laden self, will cross paths and strangely intertwine with an autumnal gothic cityscape. All the sand stuck to my body, ribbing my scalp and tangling my hair, will travel the distance between here and home.

It is odd and it is satisfying to think that what these beads of sand, those that stay in Fuerteventura and the ones I take back, will have in common is me.

The ocean imprints still stuck on my darkened skin will eventually wash off in my shower at home, spiralling, sliding, swirling around the tub until finally falling down the drain.

Before we went in for our last swim, I was staring at my feet, registering the darkness of my toes. I said to him, if I lived where my bloodline is from, this would be the natural colour of my skin. My always skin. Dark, rich brown, held and held and held by the sun.

If I was born in Tanzania, or in India, I would be different. Saltier. Oceanic not in intervals – liberating, exhilarating intervals – but always.

My lineage is one that comes from a place near water.

Instead, I am a small brown body temporarily in the warm ocean. So much time lapses in-between my visits to these warmer coastlines that each time I have to reacquaint myself. Each time, I am a stranger.

Somehow, I have come to know myself as a girl of the north. Cold, boreal forests and dark blue skies. Snowfall on mountains, ice crunching underfoot. Even after Alberta, it was Scotland. A different kind of cold, they say. A wet cold, the kind that *gets in your bones*.

My skin has fitted itself to each of these places like a chameleon.

The very last swim after blazing hot sun. Maybe one of the hottest days we experience. The water in contrast to burning skin feels impossibly cold. The dual sensations hurt and yet beyond the pain, drowning it out, is the thrill of being in chilling water. I feel my chest clamp and tighten, my shoulders tremble, going from molten to cool. Eventually we acclimatise, our bodies finding balance. The water feels warm again.

I dangle my feet, the sand somewhere unknown below me. I flip onto my back and float, my body automatically rising in the salt-water. Then I fling myself parallel to the shore and I swim.

//

We are in our own bed, in our own home, in Edinburgh. On the bus home, we passed the scaffolding of the beginnings of the Christmas market on George Street, then saw the lights strung across Princes Street Gardens from the far side. When we disembarked just past one in the morning, we walked through shimmering silver trees. The weather and its associations seemed so starkly contrasted to our past life, just hours ago. The environment so different in mid-autumn Scotland.

Awake from the adrenaline of travel, we can't sleep. On his phone, we look at photos from earlier in the day. In most, almost all, I am at the coastline with my feet in the water or I am deep in the ocean, swimming. The sun that morning, yesterday morning now, was as bright and glowing as the photos have captured. The camera sometimes points directly at the sun, my figure somewhere in the foreground.

Several photos of me – a shadow – against brilliant light.

A silhouette, water trickling toward the camera, my arms splashing saltwater into the sky.

He smiles, zooms into the photograph and says, *you look like a ghost*.

No specificity, no expressions, no lines or exact curves, no sense of tissue or muscle. Just a dark-lined figure, literally gone now, but perhaps, in ways, still there. An impression of what was.

6.1652° S, 39.1989° E

~~Trigger Notebook:~~ Fragments from the shallows of memory

I used to live in an old tenement building on Easter Road in Edinburgh. The distance between my flat and Lochend Park, the nearest green space, was 1.126 kilometres. I could gaze out of my kitchen window in its direction while washing dishes or making coffee. Although I couldn't see the loch itself, nor its abundance of waterfowl, something in my body eased knowing that it was close by. In ten minutes or less, I could arrive at Lochend Butterfly Way and be surrounded by trees and swans.

I am obsessed with the distance between spaces. By that, I mean not only geographical distances but temporal and inherited distances too. The in-betweens of things. In this context, a number as concrete as 1.126 kilometres can, at times, feel meaningless. When I slide into memory, the distance between my old flat and Lochend Park might as well be infinite. At the loch, I might look over the water's edge and feel myself transported to the Bow River, the body of water that bisects the city of Calgary. I could lean against the strong trunk of an oak tree, thriving with spring blossoms, and instead find myself under the shade of the half-blossomed crab-apple tree in the backyard of one of my several childhood homes. Moving through place dislodges memories of other places, and these remembrances swell against the boundaries of real and unreal.

If I'm honest, wild waters did not always mean so much to me. I grew up in a landlocked city, in the opposite direction from one of its watery landmarks, the North Saskatchewan River. And later, my time living in a small town in rural Alberta, overwhelmed with farmlands and rolling prairies, also instilled within me a craving for busy urban areas rather than wide open natural spaces. Perhaps every young girl is always looking elsewhere, facing the direction of something she desires and, in that process, turning away from all that she has.

~~You are hiding something here. You know that in rural Alberta, those wide open spaces did not always feel welcoming. Near the town you lived in, there might have been grasslands and birch trees, neighbouring lakes, mesmeric gardens, and long stretches of canola fields, but amidst all that space, there was not even one single mosque.~~

When I lived nearby, I walked to Lochend Park almost every day and amassed an inordinate number of field notes in my notebooks. I had just completed my PhD thesis at the University of Edinburgh – my studies were what had first brought me to Scotland – and my mind was conditioned to analysis, to note-taking. *The swans are a nostalgic tracing on the water* says one section, and it sits next to a quote from writer, musician and academic Leanne Betasamosake Simpson writing about Nishnaabeg pedagogy: '"Theory" isn't just an intellectual pursuit – it is woven with kinetics, spiritual presence and emotion, it is contextual and relational.'

Movement felt increasingly important. I walked the loop around the loch and read poetry aloud to the water birds, a practice of embodied reading that I had started during Ramadan in the spring of 2020 and have since continued. Sometimes they stuck around for the whole piece. Other times they disappeared beneath the permeable surface of the glittering loch. Or, like the swans, they threaded the near-bare trees around the water the whole time, their bodies disappearing and reappearing like a poetic refrain.

*

Memory itself is a vast, deep ocean. It holds an inherited history that I simultaneously wish was and wasn't mine. Whatever the seascape collects is, at least, honest. What enters and leaves, what lingers, what impacts its future – the sea has its own chemical and indisputable memory. A body of water does not lie. A body, however – my body – is a discursive notebook. In my attempt to chronicle the past, I gather keepsakes from my own stratified depths. Photographs, voice notes, prayers, a screengrab of my father on a video call taken on a day when he is fine and smiling, a story about my grandmother, a square of patterned fabric owned by someone now gone, any digital heirloom with a time-stamp. I convince myself I need these tethers to make sense of who I am.

In the stories that I craft for the onlooker, whether through poetry or prose, I often submerge into my memories and show kindness to every passed-down narrative I encounter. It sometimes feels like the movement toward self-love is the aim of all this creative dredging – a marker of growth and recovery. But in the version of myself that is truer, though perhaps still not true, I admit my sadness and my anger. I don't allow myself to venture into the vastness fully. I avert my gaze, even if I do so in vain. I am hurting. This history is mine and I want it, *yes*, but is it also okay to say that I don't? It is love, *yes*, but it is also pain. Even after so much unlearning of what I have internalised, of seeking out radical joy and feeling out the meaning of reclamation, there are still all those moments where I want to shrink away from my very own body.

In my palms I can only hold so much water and, when held, this water can only reflect so much of my own face. An ocean of memory, then, can only ever engulf me.

~~You are a woman who often tries to fit herself into the borderzones of the mythic norm. Of course, you fail. You ooze out of societal expectations by the very nature of being a brown woman with a history of migration, now placed within the framework of a predominantly white state. Even if quietly, you transgress. These transgressions happen in a looping pattern that continuously repeat and will repeat further still across generations. Whether you are palatable or unpalatable, you embody an amorphous, unfamiliar shape that stretches and contracts according to old and new contexts of what belongs and unbelongs. You are a woman who cannot step out of line without consequence. There is always an eye that looks through the viewfinder and there is always a hand controlling the settings. This is what it means to be a body under surveillance.~~

*

I remember hastily wriggling out of my fleece pullover. There are two other women on this stretch of beach. Their puffer jackets are sleek and black. Their two figures are far enough away that I can't tell anything specific about them, except that they are undressing too. When we enter the water, still however many metres apart, it is the ocean that connects us. Soon, we will be three bodies amongst the waves, held in the togetherness of sea swimming as passers-by look on. Water thrashes gently against all three of us, tangible and real.

Saturday, and the tide is low at Portobello Beach. Water drags along the coastline and there is a kind of morning sleepiness to the way it undulates. *Slippage*. The way the crests of waves, those small whirling peaks, come nearer and nearer until finally they break onto the shore.

In my diasporic imagination, the waves do not stop there. They keep moving, migrating into a new environment, one where they echo with their oceanic specificity in new ways. They are a little unfamiliar. Wet and silky across the sand, the waves move beyond the promenade, beyond the dog walkers, and past Crumbs of Portobello café. They cross the busy intersections, move up the stairs to the overpass bridge, and finally land next to the local pollinators in a field of wildflowers at Figgate Park. Waves and waves and waves and waves unfolding in places where another's imagination says they don't belong, moving in a way someone else might think is impossible.

In the water, the two women appear closer than they did on the shore. They look over my way and I look back. I guess that we are smiling at each other. Just us linked together in the sea on a cool summer morning.

~~You walk into a warm café. At your table, you open one of your many notebooks and find fragments of your life written untidily on the pages. You read about your swim at Portobello Beach, trying to remember the calm you felt that cool summer morning. Memory ribbons over your eyes and your vision starts to blur until you can barely see your surroundings. The girl seated next to you is eating a full Scottish breakfast and the scent of it makes you want to retch. You are suddenly too aware of the insides of your body. Your ears are too warm, and they are ringing. It feels like hot air moves into them in a constant stream that travels straight to your heart. It is winter now, but somehow you are boiling. That day on the beach, you automatically assumed the two women smiled at you. Now, only four months later, as brown bodies are dehumanised relentlessly in mainstream media,~~

~~you imagine every white stranger looks at you just a little differently than before.~~ *Slippage*. ~~The way the past slips into the bodily present and wrenches your day open like a loud December wound.~~

*

The sea is shaped by migration and migration is shaped by the sea.

There are over fourteen thousand kilometres between Edmonton and Dar es Salaam. This numerical displacement is deepened by imagination. I find a poem from six years ago wherein I envisioned the landscape of a place I hadn't ever visited. *I imagine my homeland when I am not there.* In it are descriptions of treelines and rose-ringed parakeets, of the Swahili coast likened to a body on its side. This writing was informed by research. I remember looking up the chemical make-up of soils. The most common trees. This was the kind of searching that attempted to quilt together a story riddled with gaps and unknowns. But the place in that poem is not and can never be real. It will only ever exist in the imagination of a version of myself that could only find footing in a figurative landscape. A person I no longer am. And today, I cannot articulate how far from that self I have now drifted.

In 2019, when I visited Tanzania with my father for the first time, I unearthed information about my family and family history that sits in an uncomfortable and complicated place within me. Over those three weeks, I realised I needed to look further back, beyond the generations of my grandparents, to understand the ever-present haunting of British colonialism, the migration of South Asians to East Africa, the familial disparity and loss, and all that, still, to this day, remains unspoken. The rose-ringed parakeet sounded so beautiful in my earlier poems. Now I have to admit it feels wooden and unreal while I also acknowledge that, at one point in my life, the bird was symbolic of a genuine feeling. I remind myself that both are true, that my imagined remembrance and lived experience have, together, assembled an understanding of homeland.

At Coco Beach, I think of how a young girl met these waves and waves and waves and waves long before I did. I imagine she ran along the coastline in bare feet after a long day at school. Her favourite fruit was zambarau, black plum, jamun. I imagine her fingertips were constantly empurpled with it. I imagine pinkish, sweet, slightly astringent streaks of fruit juice ebbing from her skin into the sea. The water is collecting. It collects the aftertaste of a life lived in a first home. Both girl and fruit tree have an inherited history of migration. They found themselves at this shore, carrying in them a lineage that was rooted in an elsewhere place. Always another elsewhere place.

Forty years after this imagined girl, who is a figuration of my mother, I don't run along the coastline, but I sit on a white plastic chair and watch the wild waves break onto rocks on the shore of Dar es Salaam. I am here at one of my ancestral homelands to engage with aspects of my heritage. This kind of travelling is a form of fulfilment, I think, for those of us with a history of migration. I am not sure if I feel fulfilled, exactly, but something draws me toward this coastal place that I have spent my whole life imagining. At the confluence of multiplicity, nothing is simple. But I feel peace at the cusp between land and water. I love where I am, next to family members I meet in person for the first time, in a country that had for so long tended to the childhoods of my parents. A place that knows them in a way I never will.

Looking out at the horizon, my memory decants into the water, and streaks of holographic, figurative longing reach into its depths. Even those memories that double as imaginations filter through.

Here are mirror worlds that host the inarticulable, innumerable losses tinged by forced departures. When I think of separations and connections, I am also thinking about crossings.

The sea is a poetics of movement and movement is political.

~~Yesterday at a book award ceremony, you smile and laugh and fall into step with applause. But you are lying when you agree the speeches feel powerful and political. Your life and body have always been politicised, so you are aware you have a high threshold when it comes to such things. But it is December 2023 and, for the past two months, you have seen these words: none of us are free until Palestine is free. You wonder how it is possible to give acceptance speeches about the importance of the humanities in academia and say nothing about how all the universities in Gaza have been destroyed. You wonder how it is possible to talk about reproductive rights without once mentioning Palestine, when women in Gaza are having caesarean operations without anaesthetic. On the topic of marginalised languages, you wait, somewhat hopelessly, for anyone to speak of the gross mistranslations of Arabic in the media or the misrecognition of Islamic prayer as terrorist mantra. In this room, we celebrate the power of literature, the power of words, the importance of our craft and artistry – and yet there is a glaring, painful gap in our own language when it comes to Palestine. The same day as the award ceremony, 6 December 2023, the poet Refaat Alareer is martyred.~~

*

I reconstruct a girlhood from an assortment of memories. What emerges are broad brushstrokes and fleeting images: glistening ice on a quiet side street, the alpine green of mature spruce trees, the striated greys of a young tabby cat. Of course, ultimately, I fail at this task. There is no sure methodology for deciding which tendril to keep and which to let fade away. But, still, the resulting assemblage is its own kind of ghostly truth. I think of the knowledge passed down to every iteration of myself, each created by hundreds of interpretations.

Whether ghostly or not, these details are lodged everywhere in my body, and I attempt to loosen them. I swim in a river and emerge covered in its silt. I take up running. I go for long bike rides around Leith on old railway paths. But I discover that what works best is collaboration and finding in another artist, whether in their poetry or their sculptures or their choreography, the ink that fills in an unknown missing thing. The beauty of our work together, and the frustration of it too, comes from being unable to know what that missing thing is until I am deep within the process of creation. Through the mediums of other artists, I find memories of my own past and they burgeon in random and unexpected ways.

~~Sometimes you purposefully look away. Perhaps it is an inherited shame, but then again, you think that it is too easy to always blame the past for your feeling adrift. In piecing together your childhood, you skirt around your religious upbringing. The current onslaught of Islamophobia right now, a tactic used to justify war crimes in Gaza, sends you back in time. To the recollections of an old television set being rolled into your elementary school classroom. To the furious images of 9/11 on replay by every Western media outlet. To the uncomfortable feeling of knowing your body came to represent all the fears of your young classmates. There is so much in the white space between the lines of poetry that you cannot bring yourself to say. There is so much looking away even now, right here.~~

The first time I collaborated with another artist, I wrote a poem titled after the short film *You Know it but it Don't Know You* by Welsh Gambian artist Tako Taal. The work was informed by Taal's artistic processes – by notes and photographs dotted all over her studio space – and by our conversations. We talked about fathers, saliva as artistic material, and the fractures that accompany growing up with a sense of cultural dissonance. Unsurprisingly, I came away from her studio at the Edinburgh College of Art that day with the knowledge that this poem would incorporate water, and specifically the waters between elsewhere places. The poem ends with the line *there is no irrigating a wound if that wound is the great sea*.

What I did not expect was my desire to rupture and experiment with poetic form. My response to Tako Taal's work pulled from me a different exploration, a structural one, where temporal and geographical distances – where memories, real and imagined – became physical shapes. The shape of a poem is itself an articulation, a way to create meaning. All of this reminds me of an interview with poet Bhanu Kapil about her collection *How to Wash a Heart*, where she asks the question: 'How can the poem's form – the shape that it takes, and the limits of that shape – tell the truth (or one of the truths) about what it is like to be a human being in a given world?'

In one poem from this sequence, there is a section where half the lines are in strikethrough text – still readable but crossed out. Even now, questions linger in my mind about this piece and the *there-not-there* effect on those words. How does one voice silence? And what does it mean to use a visual cue that will deliberately draw attention to the text that I supposedly want to hide away?

*

I often use the words 'nature writer' in the context of my work. In fact, I throw them around with such frequency that they start to feel meaningless, without any real definition. These words try to easily categorise a kind of work that is beyond easy categorisation. But to really understand my relationship to nature, I must delve into the past. I must acknowledge the colonial history that placed human-made borders onto living landscapes.

Often, I get the sense that nature writing's popularity aligns with its palatable broadness – the way it can easily be framed as, to a degree, apolitical. After all, if it slips into the overtly political, it is easily categorised under the framework of *ecocritical writing*. This corralling of content into genre and subgenre allows audiences to find or avoid perceived neutrality in what they read.

~~An institution says that it is apolitical, that it must remain neutral. It calls the devastation in Gaza and the murder of now over seventeen thousand Palestinians by the Israeli Military a complicated issue. We don't know enough about the conflict to comment, the director says in a private email. We have to let the board decide whether a statement is appropriate says another. You read excuse after excuse, and the underlying silence is loud in your heart. It tells you something you have always known about how bodies of colour fit into the literary culture here in the West. On the other hand, through the documentation of and dialogue around Palestine, you become more aware of ethnic cleansing throughout history and all over the world. Genocides that you said and knew very little about. In this way, you understand you, too, are the problem.~~

It is impossible to write responsibly about nature and about memory without also considering the history of empire. The land and its natural water sources are being weaponised as part of environmental warfare, or they are being exploited for capital. Often, these two things coalesce. Settler-colonialism and the legacies of imperialism around the world have shaped and revised landscapes. And as a result, they have also played a key part in establishing the various relationships a person might have to the land.

*

The sea entangles with the roots of mangrove trees. These distinctive trees grow in brackish water, saltier than most tree species can stand. Their roots, thick and tough, anchor them in place along the coastlines of Zanzibar. Depending on the tides, a mangrove forest might look like its own, independent, floating island.

When I learned that I have family in Zanzibar, I added it to my travel itinerary in 2019. It was a bewildering revelation. I had what I thought was a fairly comprehensive knowledge of at least my aunts, uncles and first cousins, even if my links beyond that were hazy and unclear. I had spent many years throughout my life imagining Dar es Salaam and Mtwara, places that I knew held my own familial roots. This recent information, however, was a newly uncovered strand of history attached to place, and I had to work its understanding into my admittedly already piecemeal sense of self. This appeal is itself perennial in nature, cropping up at intervals even when I think I have bested it, which is perhaps a condition of the second-generation immigrant.

When I visit Dar es Salaam, I find myself retrieving my first, and first lost, language after long decades of speaking only English. Kutchi is a language from the Kutch district in Gujarat, but growing up, I did not know this. It was the kind of information that I gleaned through pointed questions and archival research more recently. I still cannot trace my family's exact migration patterns on either side. A few years ago, my father told me the name of the village in India where his grandparents lived, but I was never able to find this place on a map.

~~You are reminded that you can still ask questions. You can still seek answers and find out this information. You can eventually know the paths your great-grandparents and grandparents took.~~

~~However, the last time you asked your father about India, he always dovetailed the conversation back to Tanzania, his birthplace and the home he longs for still. It does not feel right to press for answers, especially to eventually relay them back here as content. You spent years interrogating whether you were writing for the white gaze and what it means to pour out painful diasporic questions in your work. But now something in you is flourishing, some newly invigorated need to learn more and more and more in order to preserve your culture and your religion in your art, even if that means spilling out your trauma. You always say *sometimes you feel closer to your faith than others* and right now, as Islamophobic comments slither out in conversations with even your closest friends, you feel protective over your Muslim heritage.~~

I used to speak Kutchi fluently. Today, I can still understand it, keeping up with my father when we talk on the phone. However, this language shrinks in my mouth and I answer him in English. I feel like my first language dissipates the longer I am in Scotland, the longer I am away from my family. But, when I am in Dar es Salaam, Kutchi entwines around me like a scandent stem. After a few short days, I oscillate between two languages, and it is thrilling when, in my mind, I start translating Kutchi to English rather than the other way around. I think I even began to dream in it, this lost language of mine.

In Zanzibar, one of my cousins speaks only Swahili, a language unknown to me. My father is almost fluent and translates conversations between us. But when we are alone, we are unable to understand each other outside of facial expressions and body language. She and I take many photos together because doing so is something palpable that makes us feel as close as possible despite the linguistic fault lines between us.

The mangrove forest in the north is thick and alluring. When I'm on the island, after a long swim in the day, I find shelter in its shade. I learn that these trees are important for coastal ecosystems, reducing erosion where land and water meet. One day, I hear an unending creaking and I follow the sound. I am not sure what kind of omen this is, but eventually I see a giant tree snap and fall into the saltwater, clutching at mud all the while. Each stitch had been loosened for years as the mangrove was thrashed by the waves.

~~You feel your heart and body erode under anxiety and sadness. Every day, the parts of yourself that you have worked so hard to love are pulled out from under you and put on display until you begin to lose your own understanding of yourself. You find you are losing balance from the force of the unending violence you are witnessing; it feels like the ocean – often a site of violence itself – shoving itself at you and pulling you under. Equally, your body unmakes itself. It sways, falters and frays in the wake of the apathy and inaction of the world. Eventually you snap and topple into your grief, leaving only the faint watermark of your body where you once stood. Within that churning grief, you dissolve and leak out the memories that make you. In the process, you realise that~~ these ~~components of self, this terrible sadness, the huge gap left in the wake of your delusions about the system you live in,~~ all of it must become the space for us to imagine and actively make a better world. It must.

6.8165° S, 39.2894° E

Field Notes on a Beautiful and Vital Place

fragments passed down

I take my first ever photograph of Dar es Salaam. It's night outside, but there is a gentle haze in the air that emanates from lights blinking beyond the darkness. Heat comes in through the open window and catches my face. There is also the static-like sound of wind as it meets the rush of cars below. I feel both old and young at the same time. I am a scholar, a researcher, a doctoral student, holding tight my notebook and sound recorder. My mind swarms with great thinkers and theoretical concepts. Recently, I read Édouard Glissant's *Poetics of Relation* and I am obsessed with the concept of the 'errant' who rejects 'arrowlike' movement through time. I think I will capture a rhizomatic version of Tanzania, this homeland of mine, through a series of field notes over two weeks. A version that does not rely on linearity but is instead a network of overlapping and multidirectional connections or points in time. This is the hubris of someone who is starting to collect more cultural capital than she knows what to do with. Still, I am also a daughter, an emigrant, a young woman with questions. I know so very little outside of what I find in a library or in the curated collections of a sterile museum. I am estranged from the land and its memories. I no longer know the people that live here, that share blood and history with my parents. Dar es Salaam has a population of over nine million people and my father used to be one of them. Now he sits on the borrowed couch in the rented apartment I found after hours of scouring the internet. His one requirement was that we stay near the Jama'at Khana so that we are always close to the site of prayer. But we also needed something accessible with a fully equipped kitchen where we could store his insulin and other medication. My father is diabetic with bodily pain and a long medical history. I know I'll have inherited some of this in the chromosomal fragments he has passed down. I'll take this inheritance with all of the others. With the way I fit and don't fit into the shape of East Africa too.

research creation

I am here because of financial assistance I received through international project grants. As part of the application form, I had to predict what I might use the funding for and discuss what the outcomes of my research might be. The questions were impersonal, methodical and overtly interested in my output. It isn't enough to visit a homeland for the sake of visiting a homeland. At this stage of late capitalism, there must be a quantifiable artistic impact: there must be a public impact. I determine the craft techniques that are involved in excavating one's sense of self. In the form response, I write that I will produce a folio of poetry that is at least forty pages long. I will explore narrative by experimenting with long lines and represent memory through the use of fragmentation and white space. I will visit Mtwara, where my father was born, Nanyamba, where he lived as a child, and Dar es Salaam, where he spent the majority of his life before moving to Canada. I will produce tangible qualitative data, through interviews, recordings, itineraries, photographs and written field notes. Thematically, I will explore my father's return to homeland, my displacement from East Africa as a second-generation immigrant, the act of storytelling and reimagining the past, the formation of hybrid identities, and my positionality as both Muslim and Indian. My work will be deeply rooted in place. It will include intimate reflections on the natural world and how I see myself in it. This experience, I argue in my plea for subsistence, will inform and *transform* my creative practice. It will be the most innovative and experimental process I've undertaken in my career thus far. *Don't you see?* I want to say, but all that comes out is a well-rehearsed lexicon from years of literary applications and grants. *Don't you see that these poems are unique in that they can only be written here and now at this particular moment in time?*

audio recording of my father #1

`It's 22nd January 2019. The weather is fantastic. It's 28 degrees. I'm sitting here with Tim and my daughter Alycia. Today we're planning to go to the KT Shop. It has the best tea and kebabs in all of Tanzania. Beside the KT Shop was the factory where my father worked. It was a garment factory that produced children's wear. I used to eat [at the KT Shop] almost every day. My father used to eat there. My brother used to eat there. Everyone. We [couldn't] live without their kebabs and tea.`

the KT shop

On the first morning, we meet my father's best friend's son, S, who takes us around Dar es Salaam. He first brings us to Kisutu, the city's historically Indian neighbourhood. The sky is overcast and I sense heaviness in the clouds. In January, Tanzania experiences Vuli rains, otherwise known as the short rains. Between the spindly alleyways and side streets, there are emerald trees with bulbous tops. I can see ferns overflowing as we walk past light pink and orange buildings. The KT Shop itself is nondescript, a tiny hole-in-the-wall kind of place with a few people waiting outside. The yellow building is adorned only with the words KT Shop LTD in green paint above its wooden doors. If I had come alone, I might have walked right past it. From the outside, it's impossible to know the rich and long history of this place, its significance as a symbol of multiculturalism and migration. The owners are Indian immigrants from villages similar to those far back in my own lineage. Farming villages on the west coast. Inside, there are a few tables that are already filled with people devouring a mixture of Indian and Swahili dishes. The shop radiates with delicious odours. They grind all their spices at a mill before mixing them by hand into the food. The service is slow, but it's worth it. The chai smells sweet and makes my mouth water. This is an aroma that never fails to remind me of my father. Some clichés are weathered truths and need to be said. My family jokes that I used to drink chai from a bottle as a baby. I suppose that addiction is gone now. In Scotland, I'm rarely drinking sweet milky tea, so it truly is emblematic of my first *home*. Whenever I visit family in Edmonton, tea is the very first thing I'm offered. I think of it as both ceremonial and as a household staple. Food is, after all, saturated with cultural meaning and ingredients themselves tell the stories of migration. My parents overzealously show their love through food. I can only get out of a third serving of dinner if I say I'm leaving room for chai. The KT Shop uses locally sourced milk, and the chutney is made from fresh coconut. The chilis come from the earth and are fried to perfection. At a writing workshop, Nina Mingya Powles once talked about how food writing is also nature writing. I think of how these ingredients tell the story of a place that is ridged differently than elsewhere places I've lived. I think also of the colonial ecologies involving the commodity of spices, or of the now defunct groundnut factories that once dotted the inland villages of Tanzania in a disastrous scheme to extract the land for British seed oil consumption. The Indian family that owns the KT Shop didn't flee Tanzania when the country gained independence in 1961. They have tended to their home here over decades. The tea shop is an in-between place, crossing racial and cultural divides. It exists in Tanzania as much as in the migrant imagination, a fixture in the stories my father told me growing up. In a review, one customer writes, *for a lot of us, a visit to the KT Shop is about nostalgia*.

sea cliff.mov

My father is wearing a royal blue button-down shirt and standing on a grassy cliff overlooking the ocean. This water appears so often in my poetry and it did so long before I ever saw it with my own eyes. Behind my father, wide and bustling lines of foam cascade down the water's expanse. The waves are fierce and unforgiving as they crash against the rock. His mouth is moving, but the wind is billowing too hard around him. It's all I can hear: the familiar, thrashing *zzzjjjhhh* of winds at a high altitude. It's so loud that it confuses my senses and I think I can almost feel it through the screen. I wonder what he's saying. Once in a while, I hear myself laugh. I must be the one filming, close enough for the mic to catch my voice. A few minutes later, he's sitting down on a stone bench just a short distance away from the ocean. He's next to the water fountain at the nearby Sea Cliff Mall. I can hear him now. The wind has died down to a comfortable breeze. He's singing a song from an old Bollywood film with the fountain dribbling like a percussive instrument in the background. He's a remarkable singer, something I sadly haven't inherited. My father likes to be filmed and interviewed. He loves to tell us about his life. *Make sure you put all of this in your documentary*, he says to me later with a grin.

marginal note

In both the video clips and the audio recordings, my father's tongue threads together Kutchi and English and Swahili. I play back the sound over and over again, marvelling at how I can understand almost all the words of my first language as his voice travels across wind, ocean, heat and rain-soaked sky. That part of me, the past self who learned Kutchi first, feels holographic, like she is real in only certain angles, in only certain forms of light. East Africa illuminates her. I remember clearly how my languages came back to me while there. I remember how I itched to say the words out loud then, my tongue almost breaching the silence. When I listen back to these clips from my bedroom in Scotland, the sounds of Tanzania's coastal winds collapse into my life here. I feel my heart pulse with worry. My father and I were meant to go back to East Africa this January, exactly five years after our first visit. His declining health has put our travels on pause. How long before the words slip away totally? And what of him, my father, the version captured here so vibrantly against the land that birthed him? Blue on blue. My tether to language, to the past, to a form of love, retracting slowly into a faint hush, hush, *hush*.

shifting states

I want to trace Tanzania's landscape over long decades to see how it has changed. I wish, not for the first time, that I had more than merely impressions. The versions I know of this country are informed by vastly different kinds of knowledge. One of them is the Tanzania I encounter on this first and only visit. I stand on a rocky outcropping facing the Swahili coast, a coast that I had once only ever imagined, but that glitters effervescently now in front of me. It is imbued with the questions of my faith. On the shores of a figurative landscape – the Swahili coast of my mind – there exists the following artefacts: the footprints of my ancestors. Shells of prayer and the wet sands of barakat. When I was estranged from the physical landscape, I created, through poetry, a plot of land on which to sow the seeds of my belief. Both nature and literature offered me that. I look now, against the harsh sea winds and the uprising of sand, toward water. Always toward water. I love its depths, even as it unmakes the fragile truth that I once found on the page and in the lyric mode. I lean against a grey rock, my hair splitting wild against the sky, salt spray adorning my skin with its tang. If I close my eyes, I see another version: the Tanzania passed down to me over a lifetime through oral retellings. An imagined landscape that allowed me to sculpt my own social identity. In the 1970s, my parents were young. The little I have learned about their lives here is framed by childhood embellishment and fragmentation. I know each time I ask for a memory, it undergoes a metonymic slide. Nuance ends up lost to the depths of the ocean between East Africa and Canada, lost to the shrinking portal between timelines. My parents did not keep documents or diaries or letters or written words. This is a different form of my knowledge, seared into history by the note-taking European colonialists or university-affiliated ethnographers – of which I am one, I realise with some dread. I find myself reading these versions of Tanzania too. I desire more than my inheritance can provide. The past is a shifting state. Water crawls up the shore and erases the patterns we make in the sand.

audio recording #15

We have just entered Mtwara. What I see here is different. Everything is new. Now this – I don't remember this part. I didn't have this in my mind. I didn't know that this would be what Mtwara looks like. It's growing. Everything has changed. What you're looking at right now, whatever you see, it is all a new Mtwara. Before, all of this land was jungle. hotel my father Nanyamba straight Lindi Oh wow. Okay, take a picture, Alycia. Tim, look at all of this. It has all changed. Behind [us] is Lindi, another city, which I'm sure [has] also grown a lot. Look at the traffic. Korosho Ahhh. . [Laughs]. Just imagine in ten years when we come back, Mtwara will look just like Dar es Salaam.

Mtwara

We landed in Mtwara earlier that day and I was immediately taken by the greenness of the landscape under the glow of a low sun. I thought it looked and felt different to the green space of Dar es Salaam, as we passed through flat scores of land covered in long grass and interlaced with red dirt roads. Mtwara is a coastal city in the southern part of Tanzania and runs along the Indian Ocean. I think of my father spending his childhood here, in the lush southern landscape, awash with the certainty of bright green foliage and thick heat. He lived here until he was eight years old. It was less inhabited then, in the early 1960s, and like most urban regions of Tanzania, it has since undergone massive growth. Mtwara's rising population can be attributed specifically to two factors: refurbishment of its port, making it one of the three most prominent ports in Tanzania, and its increased cashew nut exports in recent years. On our way into the city, my father and our driver, J, laugh together as they peer out the open windows, chatting in a mixture of English and Swahili. There is boyish bewilderment on my father's face as we pass new roads and traffic lights and a university building, all of which didn't exist when he lived here. I wonder what he might be feeling. I wonder at the pang of his heart and at the thrill I see in his eyes. When we arrive at the shore, it begins to rain a few minutes into our coastal walk. The reprieve of cool water mixes with our sweaty skin, and my father excitedly tells us to capture it – to capture Mtwara's rain on film. Everything is special here. Everything has the potential to be a part of a new memory and must be archived. At the beach, its vistas turned grey and melancholic under the overcast sky, we meet up with H, an elderly South Asian man who has lived in Mtwara his entire life. My father got in touch with him through a connection with a family friend. H tells us that there is no longer his old Jama'at Khana here in the city. The house of prayer my father must have visited frequently as a young boy is now an abandoned building on a nearby corner. When he asks how many Ismaili Muslims still live in Mtwara, H pauses before answering. What he says surprises me, even though I know about the mass exodus of South Asians in East Africa over the course of the 1960s and 70s. Only two families.

what ifs and befores

For eighty years, Tanzania existed under first German, then British rule. If I dredge up the far past, I find that most of my family came to Tanzania as indentured labourers while others migrated under the constraints of their ancestral homes, also then under British rule. These colonial legacies over time carved out a hierarchy that privileged Indian immigrants over Black Africans and exacerbated cultural and socioeconomic differences. A proximity to whiteness allowed for their elevation in certain social, economic and political contexts, such as through means of land ownership and access to private capital. When Tanzania gained independence, these privileges were withdrawn. The country was nationalised, and the land and other private assets were returned to the government. At the same time, anti-Asian sentiment flared, and families like mine were made to leave under threat and a revocation of their rights. My parents, with their migration to Canada from East Africa, remain ambivalent about our Indian origins. They cannot easily cast their minds back to India, to the regions that held their bloodlines before they were born. It was Tanzania that contributed most notably to the formation of their identities, though it was a Tanzania imbued with Indian practices and cultures. This stronghold on Tanzania has many veins. I think one must lead back to the forced departure from a place they think of as home. Dislocation of any kind gives rise to the sediment of *what ifs* and *befores*. Forced displacement cuts through such questions to create its own specific kind of stinging wound. At times, given such a barbed and unkind history, I feel like I don't have the right to claim Tanzania as one of my own homelands. This, even despite all the love I have for this place, all the ways I know it has made me who I am. I wonder how to be *of* a country both as an agent of and a subject of the pain of colonialism, both as a daughter with East African heritage and a woman with a stranger's gaze.

the korosho tree

All along the road are medium-sized tropical evergreen trees. They catch my eye amidst the darker clusters of bushes that press against our path, those deep green blurs that are ubiquitous along the route we take as we retrace my father's history. They even draw my gaze away from the glorious trunks of trees so tall I have to crane my neck to see them in full. I'm entranced by them because of what they recall. Given a cursory first glance, the trees look broadly similar to the mountain ash or rowan trees that are prominent fixtures in Canada and Scotland. I am captivated by the throngs of reddish fruit hanging heavy on their branches, weighty cashew apples, each with a kidney-shaped seed growing out from the bottom. My father is delighted by the korosho trees too. For him, they recall the labour of my grandfather and a remembered way of life. On the beachfront is another abandoned building with several locked doors on one side. This building was once a mill, and behind the mill there is a small field where my grandfather used to tend to a modest korosho tree farm, from where you could see the rise and fall of the ocean. These trees thrive on the coastal plains of Tanzania, though they are not native to this country. The mutable patterns of green space and biodiversity here are marbled with the continent's history of conquest. In the sixteenth century, Portuguese colonialists introduced cashew plants to the neighbouring country of Mozambique for, I learn, environmental reasons, mainly in an effort to combat soil erosion. The trees spread across the east coast and formed extensive forests due to the confluence of available red clay soils and the tree's fast-growing properties. The cashew nut is now the fourth largest export in Tanzania, often cultivated in dense agroforestry systems. I hold my camera steady as it fights against the wind and take several photos of the fibrous and ellipsoidal fruit. The apples are only four or five centimetres wide. When I pick one up off the ground, its seed no longer attached, the fruit is soft and pliable. I marvel at this symbol of something that has moved across oceans over centuries. A tree that flourished in its new habitat and knitted itself deeply into the fabric of this country.

diary entry 24/01/19

I have been in Tanzania for only a few days and my phone is already filled with countless new contacts. My father is a very friendly and personable man. Two days ago, at the KT Shop, he casually introduced himself to a man sitting at one of the tables inside. This man, it turned out, had the same name as him – *Alnoor* – and went to his secondary school at roughly the same time. By the time our food arrived, the other Alnoor had invited us to his daughter's wedding, to be held at the nearby Jama'at Khana in a few days' time. As someone who can be introverted and shy at first meeting, it sometimes seems like my father and I are from entirely different walks of life. But even so, it was he who raised me. Excited (excitable), carefree, generous, talkative. These are all things I love about him. My father's motto is the borrowed phrase, 'don't worry, be happy'. He would say this to us, me and my two sisters, all the time growing up. It is only years later in Tanzania that I realise this wasn't just a catchphrase. This is his philosophy on life. He directs the course of our days this way. Don't concern yourself with minute details, don't pause and think about the negatives or what might go wrong. Be happy and trust that everything will work out by the will of God. Yet here I am, constantly thinking ahead and feeling anxious about all the things he trusts will be just fine, like arriving to places on time, and his general health. Just before this trip, he bruised the discs of his spine, and I worry about the long car rides we have been taking on the undeveloped rural roads between Mtwara and Nanyamba. We are also often speaking to strangers and going to new cities that he has only a vague recollection of. We undertake these travels without a map but with a lot of conviction that he will find his friend's old house – even after over forty years have passed and despite a few decades of erosion. But *don't worry, be happy*. The truth is, somehow, it has all been working out. My father is almost sixty now and needs assistance with a number of things in his life. But, as I have come to realise, he has many people here that are willing to assist him.

crossings.mov

There is no sound other than the rhythmic drone of the ferry as it crosses from Tanzania to Zanzibar. The journey takes an hour and a half. The light is muted even at six-thirty in the morning. The camera rests on my father as he looks out the window, his face in one hand. He looks deep in thought, pensive and perhaps even subdued. In the video captured just before this one, my father was laughing and pretending to direct the camera as if we were creating a high production film. 'I'm here with my writer and editor,' he said, gesturing for T to pan the camera over to me. It caught me smiling awkwardly and waving, looking embarrassed and not at all like someone who might be found on a film set. In the frame this time though, no one speaks or enacts anything. It's just him, shadowed as the subject of the video with a bright sky behind him, the exposure making his features somewhat dark and grainy. I capture only forty seconds, but those forty seconds are robust and full of the potential of our arrival and a noiseless calm. What is he thinking about, staring out at the ocean as we cross it? What was I thinking about watching him? Zanzibar lingers somewhere ahead in that blue expanse. I write so much about water and, when asked about this motif in my work, I often come back to the idea of crossings. These thoughts are often within a metaphorical or historical context. But here it is now, captured in just under a minute: the idea of crossing made literal. The movement we make, as a family unit, into the future, into yet another beautiful place of importance. Safia Elhillo writes, 'i am from / anywhere halved by water', and there we are, crossing from one half of ourselves to the other.

the heron!

Michamvi in the early morning, just after sunrise, is quiet and alive. My limbs are deliciously fatigued from swimming in the warm Indian Ocean. Sprawled out against one of the cliffsides along the beach, I rest my head back against stone. T draws a portrait of me in the sand. It has a surprising likeness, my dark hair drawn into a knot, my eyes drooping with a sleepy peacefulness, the wind otherwise scattering my features across the rest of the nearby land. This is, I guess, another ephemeral version of my face, another weak imprint, that I'll leave here, on the island of Zanzibar. Along the beach there are scuttling crabs of different shapes and sizes. The tiny ones are everywhere, digging their small holes, disappearing underneath the sand according to the rhythm of the tide. There are people fishing further down the coast. Their bodies catch the gleam of the sun as it reflects off the shallow trenches that, earlier, caught the saltwater as it crept up the shore and didn't let it go again. We walk toward them, though not close enough to disrupt their work. And it's there, on that slow unhurried journey, that I see the solitary heron, brushed with the remnant purples of sunrise. I want to say it is like a painting, similar to those created en plein air. But this feels like a trespass, like an imposition of tone, as if trying to write the ocean with an act that overrides it rather than tries to understand it. This scene is a form of knowledge that I don't have access to, a punctuation, a grammar, that escapes me on this short visit, even as the sinews of this island enmesh with my own drawn lines.

marginal note

Today we have our first call in thirteen days. When my father picks up, he is in the passenger seat of a car. It's bright where he is and it's dark here, seven hours into his future. I had just been watching videos of him in Tanzania, listening to his distinctive and playful voice. In one, he visits his old primary school in Nanyamba and gives an impromptu speech to all the school children at an outdoor assembly. In the five years that have passed since we went to East Africa, we often recall that day with disbelieving laughter. It was so surreal to see him there, at the podium, projecting in a confident voice all his well wishes for the hundreds of students watching him – something I myself, in all my years of teaching, still struggle to do. I mention this to him, and like always, we laugh at the situation and reminisce about it fondly. My father, after all, loves to give a speech. And then, before he leans back against the headrest, he says, *that's it*. He says he doesn't think he will be able to go back. Maybe we can go somewhere else, he adds, closer to home. But probably not East Africa. And then he changes the subject, whether purposefully or not, I can't tell.

marginal note

I don't want to lose him.

audio recording #43

`—So, you recognise this?`

`Yes, of course, Alycia, bachuli. This I know.`

44.6128° N, 124.0477° W

Impressions of an Oregon Landscape

> *I have left this page unsaid. I have withheld. What is withheld is on the left-hand page. Nine left-hand pages have already written their own left-hand pages, as you will see. They are chronic. I have withheld more than I have written.*
>
> — Dionne Brand

On our drive to the Oregon coast, we make a stop at Lake Spokane and the water is riveting. It's a 38-kilometre stretch of handsome blue in Washington state. After an eight-and-a-half-hour journey, it's a relief to see the lake's surface glitter from afar for those last minutes of our drive.

There is a feeling that washes over me when I see it. My skin prickles with the desire to go in, my chest lifts in anticipation. In that moving liquid, I see something reflected back at me: a form of love, perhaps. The poet e.e. cummings writes, 'It's always ourselves we find in the sea.' I sense in the water something that resembles a kind glance from a stranger that comes when I am otherwise feeling adrift. It promises restoration and a deep sense of calm, even if such feelings are the anaesthetisation that comes from numbness in cold water. My eyes are drawn over the long lake, noticing the many enticing spots that easily break from the shore into water. All of the places I might be able to ease myself in.

While in Brandenburg, Germany, with my friend J earlier this year, we walked along the perimeter of Hellsee during the confused weather of late winter, early spring. When she encountered the lake, enriched further by the backdrop of ancient-looking beech trees and vast floors of moss, she couldn't help it. The need to be in that body of water overcame her, despite us having left our swimsuits behind in the agreement that we would only go for a walk. She had told me once, at a different time, *the colder the water, the better*. I stayed at the edge that overflowed with tall grass and new snowdrops while she glided in. Looking at Lake Spokane, I think I understand a little of what she might have been feeling then. At the time, I merely marvelled at her daring, but now the sensations of need and impulse wash over me too.

*

i.

There is the question of what I want to numb myself from, and why with this newfound urgency. I am tired, my eyes dark with exhaustion. It would be easier to drive up the spiralling road to our campsite, rest, and come back tomorrow for a swim when the summer sun is high rather than slanted into early evening. But I am being called to the water as if it is instinctual. The movement of what looks like a strong current beckons me in with wide open arms. It promises to exonerate me from my thoughts, which are heady and anxious. They linger on the Islamophobic rhetoric I have been recently witnessing all over mainstream media, a violence that has snaked fully into my dreams, disquieting my waking and sleeping hours. At the same time, they circle around the most recent images I have of my father before I left, his body flanked by two paramedics as he disappeared into an ambulance. I feel pressed down upon from different angles, and these pressures hunch my body into itself. I want to disappear and I am riveted by the prospect of vanishing, even if only under the meniscus of water.

*

Ten years ago, in 2014, I listed all my furniture on Craigslist, packed my belongings and left Oregon, my home of two years and now forever one of my homelands. Back then, I had been falling in love across borders, held taut in that space between missing someone and being near them. A gorgeous, youthful desire that, combined with an expiring visa and the culmination of my degree, drew me back to my home province of Alberta. I turn toward T now, smiling as I steady the steering wheel of the car we've borrowed. Bess Atwell's album *Light Sleeper* plays through the speakers. I'm driving across the stunning inland landscape, flooded with the spellbinding verdure of the Columbia River valley that unfolds on our journey from Spokane to Newport.

It's impossible to know what places will leave their impression on you at the time of experience. In *The First Water Is the Body*, Natalie Diaz writes that the river is a body of water that 'remembers everything'. All my life, I have lived in cities bisected by rivers, where buildings are parted by the rhythm of streaming water, and I have been unknowingly changed by them. On our drive, I think less about fathomless, mercurial expanses of water – like the ocean and its narratives of exile – and more about water as a reflective place that remembers everything, where one is able to re-encounter herself and her wayward thoughts.

In her long poem, Diaz also quotes Toni Morrison, who writes, 'all water has a perfect memory and is forever trying to get back to where it was'. I am returning to Oregon after a decade, travelling on the lush ecological map that emerges alongside a river gorge. I am following water to the water. I am following water to the memory of myself. Nostalgia plagues me, and so I have dedicated my life to pinning down the ephemeral qualities of the past in my art. Like water, I am forever trying to return.

*

ii.

This trip is born from the strong desire to go back to a rose-tinted moment on my timeline. A period wherein I discovered how to love my body for the first time, a body which I had until then treated unkindly, even hated – its brownness, its heaviness, its stretch marks, its queerness. All of this was then cherished and shown intimacy, too, by someone else. At the same time, I was also overcome in the throes of artmaking and I was given, for the first time, the resources to explore my creative voice as much as I desired to. In memory, my life in Oregon sits at the hinge of two conflictual periods: the child who was first wounded by racial and religious unrest around 9/11; and the woman who I am now. The woman who is retraumatised and embarrassed by the raw emotions that leak into everything she does. This is, after all, a world that constantly imposes its prescriptions on how I should and shouldn't act.

*

iii.

And here is where the text breaks apart and thus so does the persona. In *The Blue Clerk*, Dionne Brand creates an enthralling metaphor where the author chooses only seemingly presentable, beautiful things to include in her writing. What is unsaid, the marginal notes, the unspoken and resisted, is handled instead by the figure of the clerk who attends to them on the 'left-hand pages', the pages of all that is withheld. In her transformative work, the two personas encounter one another. I want this essay to be about the extravagant and ecologically stunning impressions I have of the Oregon coast, whether in the past or present. That is why, on the page, I feel I must withhold the news I receive while writing. The news that jars me out of any sense of peace within poetry or art and interrupts the rhythm of my narrative storytelling. The news that ruptures the lie I tell myself about the healing properties of water. The news that now flows, too, in Lake Spokane, evaporating off my body and into those small freshwater waves that will remember everything.

*

I remember Newport as fervent grey in colour and loud with the tender barks of sea lions. At least one of these things is still true. The coast remains cool and shrouded in the mist that is archetypal of the Oregon coast. I look out at the tableau of grey on grey, water and sky blending together and forming a plane that is disrupted only by the shapes of fishing boats. A chill crawls up my arms and I put on my coat as T and I walk toward the things we remember: the Candy Shoppe with stacks of saltwater taffy and the pier where the male sea lions are always sunbathing.

The docks are quiet and empty. The sea lions, it seems, have already migrated for the breeding season. Female sea lions don't typically come as far north as Oregon and, for the month of July, male sea lions head south to California to mate. I lean over the railing, dismayed. I have never seen the docks empty. I feel like I am in the shell of an old memory. It's June and inland temperatures rise steadily, reaching heights that were unfathomable even just ten years ago. A recent study found that, over the last twenty years, juvenile salmon migration timing has changed due to climate change. I wonder if the sea lions are beginning to migrate sooner, following their food source to the Channel Islands earlier and earlier every year.

Later, at South Beach, we unwrap our taffy and settle next to the shore, eyes focused on the horizon. Draped lazily over the sand, I read *Crying in H Mart* by Michelle Zauner, a writer and musician who was raised in Eugene, Oregon. It reminds me of when I lived there too, with its references to the Willamette River and its vibrant imagery of green space, volcanic rock, and the omnipresent pine trees. I think of the people I crossed paths with in that timeline, and how some remain my close friends though I rarely get to see them in real life. Reading this book here is a coincidence that I love, even as it draws closer my homesickness while simultaneously flinging the past further from my grasp.

*

iv.

It feels false to hold together personal and global griefs, even though it's true that both riddle my heart and breach my sense of self. In my small world there is a door where individual sadnesses and larger griefs swing through without knocking. The darkness bleeds and entangles. Together with the anticipatory grief of illness, there is also the hostile world. I witness race riots, rising fascism, live-streamed genocide, and environmental degradation that disproportionately affects the most marginalised. I witness how the bodies on the front line of decolonisation are the bodies that are most vulnerable. I want to escape the present tense. My return to the Pacific Coast is born from the mistake of believing the past is innocent. Of course, it isn't, and even if it were, one can never truly return. The self undergoes constant change. As the environment itself changes, so too does the speaker.

*

I try on the wetsuit for the very first time. Before I ever dared to dip into cold waters and before spiralling cool aches up my spine ever meant anything to me, I spent those earlier years walking along the Oregon coast and observing the tempestuous ocean from afar. I understood that the crawling saltwater carried a symbol with it and knew that the roar of waves could filter away the noise in my mind. Even then, I wanted to be the kind of woman who found herself on the shores of something I thought was wild, who was able to get close to and make skin contact with the mythology of the Pacific Coast. I was drawn to its varied landscapes of piercing rocks, sand dunes and opulent forest, and its remarkable geological history that left marine terraces and natural rock arches in its wake.

I think back to those years and how I lived, in some ways, with abandon. But I also didn't swim, I think now, as I zip up the tight wetsuit over my body and gaze at the waves of the ocean head on. The tide is out and the shallows continue over a long stretch into the depths of the sea. I see the direction of the water tilt when a giant wave encounters one of the equally giant rocks burgeoning from the saltwater. It crashes furiously a few seconds later. I look back at the shore over my shoulder. All the sunbathers and families are far away, becoming tinier specks as I tread into deeper water. I feel alone here, in a way that is freeing rather than lonely. I realise that, over the years, I have become more unafraid. I have found a strong shelter in my awareness of self, in the person I have grown into or otherwise found through the world I create in my art. And I am more in tune with my body, even if most new discoveries of and about it are gentler as I age.

*

v.

How to contend, then, with the way I flinch at photographs? I notice in them too keenly how my figure changed over the early months of 2024, becoming a different shape under the forces of stress and despair. I turn away from the camera. It's not only my body; I know my perception of my physical self intertwines with ingrained cultural and societal expectations of beauty that I am constantly trying to free myself from with varying degrees of success. It's also the lack of care I have shown myself emotionally in the face of that despair. The deterioration, too, of my mental health that is then reified in my expressions, my unwillingness to smile broadly, my gravitation to the very corners of the frame. I suppose I have over time found a stronger kind of self-love and acceptance, but there is still so much to learn and unlearn about care.

*

Soon after I left Oregon in 2014, I wrote a poem about Cape Perpetua. I was moved by the landscape and looked toward modernist nature poets like James Wright and Elizabeth Bishop for inspiration, writers who I felt captured the natural world in their stanzas. In turn, Cape Perpetua became intimately entwined with my expressions and memories of the Oregon coast. It became a placeholder for all that I adored about the coastal weather and its dreamlike qualities. Eventually, a metaphorical version of it began to replace the literal landscape in my mind.

I wrote about how heavy clouds moved in and ensorcelled the cliffs, covering the ocean below and surrounding the coastal rainforest in mist. I remember even at the crest I couldn't make out the topographical wonders of the cliffs ahead, though on a clear day it should be possible to see over a hundred kilometres of the

Oregon coastline. I remember I felt utterly blanketed, and nestled within that cocoon were feelings of safety and awe.

In the early morning, we head from our campsite at South Beach toward Cape Perpetua. The headland is forested and, to reach the top of the bluff, we take a steep trail through the trees. The land here is part of the Siuslaw National Forest, which in its entirety is 630,000 acres. The day is clear and the sky is a crystallised blue, unlike the Cape Perpetua of my memories and in my art. This is not the return I imagined, and I feel exposed without the light brume that I remember.

*

vi.

The forest around Cape Perpetua reveals a history entangled with the Alsea people as far back as six thousand years ago. They named the area Halaqaik. Cape Perpetua is the moniker of the land after it was stolen by the British, christened as such by the euphemistically labelled British 'explorers' after Saint Perpetua in 1778. The name Halaqaik suggests that, once, the landscape was 'uncovered', 'open' or 'exposed', resembling coastal prairies rather than allotted with its now towering trees. The change in landscape runs parallel to the change in human caretaking and land use around Cape

Perpetua. Compositional and spatial ecological changes reflect how the Alsea people were forcibly and violently removed from the area that formed their homes.

*

vii.

Canada, where I grew up, is a settler-colonial nation with a similarly violent history. Today, there remains ongoing erasure in the reinforcement of legislature that continues to influence land use and displace resources, and in the form of cultural genocide that has suppressed Indigenous knowledges and languages. I think of my early education in poetry, how I was taught persistently that good literature extended from the English canon, the verses of Shakespeare and Milton. What I didn't know then was that these exclusively white, Western/European authors – this colonial syllabus – clouded the works of Black and Indigenous poets, and poets of colour. This literary wound feels small in the face of greater devastations but still it tells something of the story of how I, and others, came to seek

alignment with institutions and
establishments over people. This
is something that I am presently
working on understanding better
about myself.

*

Cape Perpetua is a globally important bird area and, in the past few years, I have taken up very occasional birdwatching. Slung around my neck are my binoculars, which I lift to my eyes whenever I see even the faintest of movements. Though there could be endangered birds from Antarctica, the Arctic, Japan or New Zealand in the canopies, I rarely make out any shapes through the lenses except small blackbirds and bright blue Steller's jays.

As we climb up to the acme, which rises eight hundred feet above sea level, we ascend along a path dense with flora. I notice that the names of the man-made trails are beautiful, like poetry. One is called *whispering spruce trail*, which indicates something about the area and its atmosphere, how one might hear the wind rustle through the spruce trees that now make up large swathes of the headland. As we walk, I think about what I might name the trails I've made or left over my own lifetime; the thorny trail from Vilna to Edmonton along the interior plains, or perhaps the scree I fearfully struggled over on Mount Yamnuska. *Twinning lodgepole pine trail* or *slippery silver rock walk.* I do it too often, giving into the impulse to metaphorise nature as a representation of myself. It's an uncomfortable urge to want to leave a mark, a name, a footprint, on a place.

Climbing up the switchbacks with glimmers of light breaking through tree trunks reminds me of the many hikes I once took up Spencer Butte in Eugene. This memory ebbs into another: climbing Arthur's Seat in Edinburgh. Both cities are marked by their own hills. I realise I can't remain in my thoughts about the fog of Cape Perpetua any longer. My muscle memory unearths too many moments beyond that snapshot of time.

*

viii.

For the past few years, I have found it increasingly difficult to read and to write. This has fractured my sense of identity. Every time I try, I have a severe bodily response that is akin to the urge to vomit. This summer, though, I find respite in those moments my mind wanders into areas of artmaking, of poetry, of its own accord. There is no force or will or pleading involved. This kind of opening seems to happen most often here, in nature. It delights me when, walking along Oregon's scenic corridor with the endless ocean in view, my mind crosses the threshold into new and surprising vocabulary and trilling sound. I'm surprised by this creeping eagerness to put words to paper again. I realise that part of my current experiment to return to the Pacific Coast, to experience even the ghosts of the past, comes from the hope of retrieving my love for art again. I want to dislodge the bad habits and capitalist ideas of production I have since absorbed. I want to remember and hold close the feeling of what it was like when I first invited myself to speak through the page.

*

As the month turns over into July and T and I head further south, we give ourselves over to the heat. It's hot all day and night. I'm normally attuned to the cold earth beneath me while sleeping in a tent, often chilled despite the season, but the blazing weather tamps on us from all angles, above and below. I chuck aside my sleeping bag and we keep the tent flaps open at night.

In the morning, on our way to Siltcoos River Trail, we see fire danger signs along the road. The arrow still points toward the middle of the sign at the word *high*, though I think, as we head south to eventually cross the border into California, that arrow will soon tip into *very high* or even *extreme* territory. The wildfires of the Pacific Northwest have sent thick strokes of smoke into Alberta for as long as I can remember. In some areas during our drive there are ripples of deadwood forests, their trunks a black and splintered map exposing the tear of an old forest fire.

I haven't kayaked for some time. It was T who first introduced me to experiencing the water this way all those years ago, and it has since become one of my favourite outdoor activities. In 2015, I joined a Dragon Boat team and paddled with new strength across Glenmore Reservoir in Alberta for two summers. I never go very far out into the water when swimming, not like my friend G who I once watched swim across the entire expanse of Loch Meiklie and back again in the Scottish Highlands. But from a vessel propelled by different muscles in different ways, I am offered the chance to see beautiful waters further away from the margins of the land.

The river canoe trail is a three-mile paddle between Siltcoos Lake and the Pacific Ocean. On the map outside the kayak rental building, we see that the route is fairly straight with some bends that lead toward campsites or day areas, like the lodgepole picnic area. We choose a tandem kayak day rental, which will allow us to arrive together at the shores of the coast and stay there for a while. I notice with interest that some areas are marked red, signalling that they are roped off for snowy plover nesting season through March to September.

There is the option, too, to kayak instead at Siltcoos Lake, Oregon's largest coastal lake, but ultimately I decide that would be too advanced for me. In Wales two summers ago, we camped at Llyn Gwynant Campsite close to the foot of Snowdon. The campsite was also near a popular boating spot. I had confidently, then, agreed to go up the river, Afon Glaslyn, and kayak into the lake. I remember how the robust waters ushered us further and further out, and the fear I felt in that strong drag still shivers in me when I think back to that day. Lately, I'm trying to accept the limits of my body and find pleasure in moments of stasis, also discarding the negative associations I once felt around words like *limit* and *stasis*. This instead of always trying to reach forward, move ahead, go further, higher, faster, as if success and ambition are more important than the attempt at something and the enjoyment of trying.

On the water, I am enrapt by the cattails and willowy thickets on the river's fringes. My chest buzzes with the sheer wonderment I feel looking into the forests on either side of me, trees that eventually blend and become sand dunes before the river unfolds into a wide estuary that opens onto the sea. I'm in the front of the kayak, with T behind me, and I laugh when our paddles knock into each other. We sometimes inadvertently bob toward the edges of the river or toward the great trunks of fallen trees that have only the tiniest layer of water over them, and so must be avoided lest we get stuck.

We are leisurely as we move ahead, catching sight of several marsh wrens on our way to the glorious sight of the ocean. It emerges ahead of us like the heavenly sky, spanning forever beyond the thin band of the river. Perhaps the sight I love the most, though, is the heron. I spot her first, near the marshy wetland and amongst yellow flowers. And when we are close, so close, she flies from one side of the river to the other. Her wings move slowly, enchantingly, as she skates through the air. I have never seen a heron like that before. We were so near, I think then, so much a part of the ecosystem.

*

ix.

I write notes on my phone as we travel along the Oregon coast. Most list the birds we see – the heron, but also vultures and cormorants and guillemots and gull chicks. T thinks we see a black-footed albatross, but I think it might be a south polar skua. It is unlikely, though, to be either of these things. In one note that I compose while resting at a place called Secret Beach, I write that *revisiting Oregon is for the most part beautiful and I love it, but it is also a reminder that I can't actually go back*. Being here has only made clearer the realisation of how much I have changed. I have returned to several locations and found in each little jagged moments of love. Still, retracing my steps has made me confront what is different and also realise there are parts of myself I don't want to look at. My melancholy feels unseemly next to the names of birds and the illustrations of riveting waters. I consider removing all these interpositions, deleting all the worry and anxiety and self-criticism from the larger essay. I consider removing those parts of myself that exist outside of my filtered and meditative love of nature.

*

The night before we drive to Crater Lake, I wake up in the pitch-black darkness. I think I hear emergency helicopters and the sounds of heavy machinery, or perhaps even a churning industrial train. I also think I can smell smoke. I wake up T and say that I think there's a forest fire nearby. He reminds me the forest rangers would have let us know if we were in danger. They are only a few campsites away. Even so, I slept uneasily after that. When we wake up in the morning and begin our early journey, there are extreme fire warnings all along the highway, big boards propped up against the green blur of lodgepole pine. My dream mind and dream body, perhaps because of the accumulated heat and dryness seeping through my porous skin all night, knew the truth before my waking self.

Crater Lake is part of the Cascade Range, which is made up of volcanic and non-volcanic mountains that extend from California to British Columbia. The eight-to-ten-kilometre caldera was formed by the massive eruption of Mount Mazama around 7,700 years ago and, over hundreds of years, the basin filled with only rainwater and snowmelt. It's the deepest lake in the US, with profoundly clear waters that take on a striking, now representative, cobalt blue. I remember that unforgettable blue. Crater Lake is the kind of natural wonder that leaves you breathless, that makes you pause, makes you still. Walking around the trail of the crater, through the ridge-top forest, is slow and hypnotic because it requires so much stop and start. It is a deep, ellipsoidal vat of blue, and yet it looks marvellously different with every glance and small movement.

For fun, we try to recreate a photo from a decade ago. I am wearing the exact same blue zip-up fleece, the colour as bright as ever, though it fits more snugly now. I pose just the same, sitting on a stone bench, my head turned slightly to peer at the lake, one leg crossed over the other. There are the same clusters of trees in the frame, the same crests and mounds and darknesses and colours atop the caldera's walls. Though we notice there is less snow, and perhaps the treeline has moved too.

The photos are almost exactly the same, though taken ten years apart. Through the processing and flattening of the image, my blue sweater takes on an identical hue to the splendour of the water. And somehow, still, I look at the recent version and find faults – with myself, with my posture and other minor details that I know no one else would see. I wonder how much I might love *this* version ten years from now.

In *Siddhartha*, there is the question: 'Have you also learned that secret from the river; that there is no such thing as time?' The river, Hesse goes on to say, is everywhere at the same time.

It always feels hard for me to appreciate the present, to always want to dip into the iridescent river and access another moment in time, to approach the water as a way to escape rather than to savour. Perhaps, like Virginia Woolf says in her diary, 'I can only note that the past is beautiful because one never realises an emotion at the time.' But, staring at the gleaming lake, a wonder of the world, I feel something in me settle. I put away the identical photos and, with that gesture, push aside my anxiety of never living up to some idolised version of myself, or version of the world.

Instead, I notice that the words I'm jotting down every day become longer, more imagistic and sculpted. I find my poet's language coming back to me, or perhaps reawakening from where it has lain dormant. I realise the landscape, these deeply felt and remembered impressions, the invitation to slow down and linger in the world, helped to unstop the ink of my pen.

I turn to T. I hold his face in my hands. I notice the soft lines coming into place, probably in similar places to the soft lines emerging on my own body. I brush my fingers across the scattering of white hairs in his beard. I smile at the changes, so unnoticeable day by day.

This reminds me that there is beauty in the selves we become, that there is so much to love right here, right now.

Epilogue

Every Memory Is the First Memory

My knees are wet at the boundary line
where land and water meet,
where I hold up a mirror to the ocean
and sieve saltwater for traces
of my migrant history.
A wave is borderless, a wave collapses
past and present and future.
A wave is a wound that won't heal,
A wave is a wound that stores prayer –
thirty-three beloveds and recitations,
thirty-three beads of my tasbih
quivering like a mantra in the wind.
The water anthologises every tremor,
every swell, departure and act of love
until it fades into inheritance.

The act of leaving sometimes feels
like submerging one long unnumbered
river into another river's shape.
I am a woman riven with porous
shoreland and wet with ghosts.
My ancestor's past filters through the gaps
of a temperate forest's trees,
and the sediment of selective history
is an ocean that reflects

the very first memory –
My ancestor's gap filters through my gaps.
The past opens and becomes.
It lifts like fog over the threshold

and slips free—

Acknowledgements

Writing *Shorelines* has made me feel closer than ever to the people who made me. First, thank you to my family – my father, my mother, my sisters – who mean the whole world to me. I love you all so much. Thank you to my extraordinary partner and soulmate, Timothy Phillips, and to the Phillips family. Thank you to my aunts and uncles, my cousins, my nephews, and to my ancestors who I never met, but who live within these pages too. *Shorelines* is a book about us, but I hope it also feels like a book *for* us.

I was born and raised in amiskwaciwâskahikan, or Edmonton, Alberta, and grew up on Treaty 6 territory, the homelands of Indigenous peoples including the Cree, Nakota Sioux, Blackfoot, Métis, Dëne Sųłıné and Saulteaux peoples. In *The Big Melt*, nêhiyaw poet Emily Riddle writes about the gruffness of the prairies and of non-prairie softness. My relationship to land and nature – to the prairies that are so important to me and helped make me who I am – began here, as a second-generation immigrant and as a settler in Canada. I want to acknowledge how treaty land interweaves with the chapters in this book, as well as directs my actions and attention toward Land Back movements across the world.

I'm grateful for the friendship and support of many loved ones in my life. Nicole Lachat and Adriana Oniţă, we have been through so much together, over so many years. Thank you for being there for all of it. Thank you for your love and your care. Thank you for letting me cry on your shoulders. When I look ahead to the future, you're both always beside me.

Thank you to my precious collaborators in the *fieldnotes collective*: Pratyusha, Jessica J. Lee and Nina Mingya Powles. I'm so grateful for all the advice you gave me on this book, and all the conversations we had about the nebulous genre of nature writing. Our friendship, our meals together, our wonderful travels and our group chat are truly a lifeline. Dawn Muenchrath, and Laura Schoenberg, thank you for countless Zoom calls and coffees in Kensington, for our weekend of leisurely hikes and tasty s'mores and, of course, for sharing your writing with me. Jay Gao, thank you for helping me build a community in Scotland, and thank you, especially, for all your spicy literary takes.

Shorelines would not exist without my wonderful friends and literary community: Shasta Hanif Ali, Sarah Anderson, Dean Atta, Crystal Bennes, Jess Brough, Anthony V. Capildeo, Ezra Carlsen, J.R. Carpenter, Dave Coates, Hannah Copley, Titi Farukuoye, Rebecca Ferrier, Nadine Aisha Jassat, Tom Jeffreys, Jessica Gaitán Johannesson, Mihir Khandekar, Alyson Kissner, Hannah Lavery, Amy LeBlanc, Aileen Lees, Marjorie Lotfi, Éadaoín Lynch, Michael McDermit, Helena Fornells Nadal, Christina Neuwirth, Alyssa Ogi, Andrés N. Ordorica, Jeda Pearl, Joe Mungo Reed, Jayme Ringleb, Zain Rishi, Mo Tonsy, Jacques Tsiantar, Anna and Stig Viaene, Elsa van der Wal and Jessie Widner.

Victoria Chang, thank you for your advice on so many of these pieces. *Shorelines* transformed under your mentorship. It was a joy and honour to work with you on this book. And Bhanu Kapil, you have been such an inspiration for so long. Thank you for your time, your spirit, and your writing – which you'll probably notice has been a key influence on these pages.

Thank you to my friends and mentors who advised on this book or otherwise helped me develop as a writer and scholar: Bert Almon, Olga Costopoulos, Alan Gillis, Kendel Hippolyte, Jane King Hippolyte, Garrett Hongo, Sarah Howe, Shawna Lemay, Sigrid Nama, Sandeep Parmar, and my late mentor and teacher, Derek Walcott.

Gratitude to Moniack Mhor and the poets involved with the Here and Now Residency: Tolu Agbelusi, Genevieve Carver, Chika Jones, Heather Parry, Edwige Renée-Dro and Amanda Thomson. Much of this book was written during our time together in the Scottish Highlands and in Ghana. I'm so glad to have made lifelong friendships with all of you. And thank you to Noreen Masud for the inspirational *A Flat Place* and for your writing prompts, which evoked so much for me.

Thank you to Scottish Book Trust for the invaluable support of the Ignite Fellowship, and to the Canada Council for the Arts and the Calgary Arts Development for providing funding for this work – and others – over the years. Thank you also to the CBC Poetry Prize and the Banff Centre for Arts and Creativity for providing the beautiful writing studio that I refer to in these pages. Thank you to *Gathering: Women of Colour on Nature* (404 Ink), *Salted Words* (Salted Books), *New Ohio Review* and *Critical Muslim* for first publishing versions of these pieces. And a little shoutout to The Nook (formerly OQO) on Leith Walk in Edinburgh for providing the physical space and the caffeine necessary to write this book.

Shorelines is especially indebted to the Nan Shepherd Prize and to judges Jason Allen-Paisant, Peggy Hughes and Claire Ratinon. I can't express how much it means that you gave me and my writing this chance. I'm so grateful for my agent, Caro Clarke at Portobello Literary, and my editors Helena Gonda and Claire

Reiderman at Canongate. Your patience and kindness, your guidance and your incredible editorial feedback during the making of this book are so appreciated. I am keenly aware that *Shorelines* wouldn't be what it is without you. Thank you, thank you, thank you.

Works Cited

Adnan, E. *Shifting the Silence*. Nightboat Books, 2020. (Second printing, 2021.)

Ahmed, S. *Strange Encounters: Embodied Others in Post-Coloniality*. Routledge, 2000.

Ali, A.S. (ed.). *Ravishing DisUnities: Real Ghazals in English*. Wesleyan University Press, 2015.

Ali, K. *Northern Light: Power, Land, and the Memory of Water*. Milkweed Editions, 2021.

Allen-Paisant, J. 'On Blackness and Landscape: Reclaiming Time.' *PN Review*, 47(3), 2021.

Alsadir, N. *Fourth Person Singular*. Liverpool University Press, 2017.

Ball, R. 'Light Work.' *Radicle: Decolonising Nature Writing*. Substack Newsletter, 2024

Barrera, J. *On Lighthouses*. Two Lines Press, 2020.

Bathurst, B. *The Lighthouse Stevensons*. Harper Perennial, 1999.

Behrooz, A. *BFFs: The Radical Potential of Female Friendship*. 404 Ink, 2023.

Belcourt, B.-R. *NDN Coping Mechanisms: Notes from the Field*. House of Anansi Press, 2019.

Brand, D. *The Blue Clerk*. McLelland & Stewart, 2019.

Brand, D. *A Map to the Door of No Return: Notes to Belonging*. Random House Canada, 2001.

Burnett, L. *Skin memories: from Stone Arthur to Nab Scar - a loop above Grasmere*. Available at: https://scree.org.uk/routes/skin-memories. 2022 (Accessed: 2024).

Carpenter, J.R. *This is a Picture of Wind* (First edition). Longbarrow Press, 2020.

Carson, A. *Plainwater: Essays and Poetry*. Alfred A. Knopf, 1995.

Chang, V. *Dear Memory: Letters on Writing, Silence, and Grief*. Milkweed Editions, 2021.

Chari, A. 'Exceeding Recognition.' *Sartre Studies International*, 2004, 10(2), pp. 110–122.

Cohen, R., & Fischer, C. (eds). *Routledge Handbook of Diaspora Studies*. Routledge, 2019.

Coulthard, G.S. *Red Skin, White Masks: Rejecting the Colonial Politics of Recognition*. University of Minnesota Press, 2014.
cummings, ee. 'maggie and milly and molly and may.' Forward Arts Foundation. Available at: https://forwardartsfoundation.org/poemday/maggie-and-milly-and-molly-and-may/. (Accessed: 2024).
DeLoughrey, E., & Handley G.B. (eds). *Postcolonial Ecologies: Literatures of the Environment.* Oxford University Press, 2011.
Diaz, N. *Postcolonial Love Poem*. Graywolf Press, 2020.
Diaz, N. 'The First Water is the Body.' *Emergence Magazine*. Available at: https://emergencemagazine.org/poem/the-first-water-is-the-body/. (Accessed: 2024).
Dillard, A. *The Abundance: Narrative Essays Old and New*. Ecco, 2016.
Dixon, A. *The Loneliness Files: A Memoir in Essays*. Tin House, 2023.
Duyne, E.V. 'Diary of a Pilgrimage: Marking the Gravesite of Assia and Shura Wevill.' *Literary Hub*. Available at: https://lithub.com/diary-of-a-pilgrimage-marking-the-gravesite-of-assia-and-shura-wevill/. 2022 (Accessed: 2024).
Education, U.C. for S. *Center for Science Education, Thunderstorms | Center for Science Education*. Available at: https://scied.ucar.edu/learning-zone/storms/thunderstorms (Accessed: 2024).
Elhillo, S. *The January Children*. University of Nebraska Press, 2017.
Elkamel, S. 'Half Lives and Long Drives: An Interview with Anne Carson and Robert Currie.' *Literary Hub*. Available at: https://lithub.com/half-lives-and-long-drives-an-interview-with-anne-carson-and-robert-currie/. 2021 (Accessed: 2024).
Esselborn, S. 'Environment, Memory, and the Groundnut Scheme: Britain's largest colonial agricultural development project and its global legacy.' *Global Environment*, 2013, 11: pp. 58–93.
Fanon, F. *Black Skin, White Masks:* Forewords by Homi K. Bhabha and Ziauddin Sardar. Pluto Press, 2008.
Frank, C. 'Fragmented Realities: Movement, Pleasure and Surveillance.' *Tongues* ed. Rehana Zaman. PSS Books, 2018.
Fraser, W. 'The time is now to rename Tunnel Mountain.' *Rocky Mountain Outlook*. Available at: https://www.rmoutlook.com/vox-populi/letter-the-time-is-now-to-rename-tunnel-mountain-4216953. 2021 (Accessed: 2024).
Glissant, E. (Translated by Betsy Wing.) *Poetics of Relation.* University of Michigan Press, 2017.
Gopal, P. *Insurgent Empire: Anticolonial Resistance and British Dissent*. Verso, 2020.
Hesse, H. *Siddhartha*. Adelphi, 2022.

Hikmet, N. 'Things I Didn't Know I Loved.' *Academy of American Poets*. Available at: https://poets.org/poem/things-i-didnt-know-i-loved. N.d. (Accessed: 2024).
Hill, P. *Stargazing: Memoirs of a Young Lighthouse Keeper*. Canongate Books, 2004.
Kapil, B. *The Vertical Interrogation of Strangers*. Kelsey Street Press, 2001.
Kapil, B. *Schizophrene*. Nightboat Books, 2011.
Kapil, B. *Ban en Banlieue*. Nightboat Books, 2015.
Lauterbach, A. *The Night Sky: Writings on the Poetics of Experience*. Penguin Books, 2005.
Lee, J.J. *Two Trees Make a Forest: On Memory, Migration and Taiwan*. Virago, 2020.
Lee, J.J., et al. *this too is a glistening*. Bitter Melon 苦瓜, 2024.
Lunden, J. 'Evidence, in Track Changes.' *Diagram*. Vol. 17, Issue 3 (no date).
Maitland, S. *Gossip from the Forest: The Tangled Roots of our Forests and Fairytales*. Granta Books, 2013.
Meghji, S. 'Rediscovering a Lost Piece of Ismaili History — First Steps in the Migration of Tanzanian Ismailis to Canada.' *Simerg Magazine*. Available at: https://simerg.com/literary-readings/rediscovering-a-lost-piece-of-ismaili-history-first-steps-in-the-migration-of-tanzanian-ismailis-to-canada/. 2014 (Accessed: 2014).
Nezhukumatathil, A. 'Landscape and Literary Culture.' Associlation of Writers and Writing Programs, 2022.
Oliver, M. *Upstream: Selected Essays*. Penguin Books, 2019.
Parmar S., Kapil, B., and Ramayya, N. *Threads*. Clinic, 2017.
Paroo, A. 'Aga Khan III and the British Empire: Ismailis in Tanganyika, 1920–1957.' York University Libraries, 2012.
Phillips, C. 'Among the Trees' in *The Language of Trees: A Rewilding of Literature and Landscape* by Holten, K. Tin House Books, 2023.
Pollock, A. and Kapil, B. 'How To Wash A Heart: An Interview with Bhanu Kapil.' Liverpool University Press Blog. Available at: https://liverpooluniversitypress.blog/2020/04/27/how-to-wash-a-heart-an-interview-with-bhanu-kapil/. 2020 (Accessed: 2024).
Posmentier, S. *Cultivation and Catastrophe: The Lyric Ecology of Modern Black Literature*. Johns Hopkins University Press, 2017.
Powles, N.M. *Small Bodies of Water*. Canongate Books, 2021.
Pratyusha. *bulbul calling*. Bitter Melon 苦瓜, 2020.
Pullan, B. 'These Banff Mountains Had Indigenous Names.' *Gripped Magazine*. Available at: https://gripped.com/profiles/these-banff-mountains-had-indigenous-names/. 2021 (Accessed: 2024).

Ball, R. 'Light Work.' *Radicle: Decolonising Nature Writing*. Substack Newsletter, 2024.

Ramayya, N. *States of the Body Produced by Love.* Ignota, 2019.

Riddle, E. *The Big Melt*. Nightwood Editions, 2023.

Shan, X.Y. 'To That Silence, I Told Everything.' Granta 162, Essays & Memoir, 9 February 2023. Available at: To That Silence, I Told Everything | Xiao Yue Shan | Granta Available at: https://granta.com/to-that-silence-i-told-everything/. (Accessed: 2025).

Shepherd, N. *The Living Mountain*. Canongate Books, 2019.

Shin, S.Y. *Unbearable Splendor*. Coffee House Press, 2016.

Simpson, L.B. 'Land as pedagogy: Nishnaabeg intelligence and rebellious transformation.' *Decolonization: Indigeneity, Education & Society*, 2014, Vol. 3, No. 3, pp. 1–25.

Solnit, R. *Wanderlust: A History of Walking*. Granta Books, 2001.

Stephenson, R. *Records of a Family of Engineers*. Chatto & Windus, 1912.

Swensen, C. *On Walking On*. Nightboat Books, 2017.

Taal, T. *You Know it but it Don't Know You.* Talbot Rice Gallery, 2020.

Taylor, B. 'Sad Queer Books: Why My Melancholy Heart Loves Joan Didion.' them. Available at: *Why My Sad Queer Heart Loves Joan Didion | Them*. Available at: https://www.them.us/story/sad-queer-books-joan-didion. 2018 (Accessed: 2025).

Tejpar, A. 'The Migration of Indians to Eastern Africa: A Case Study of the Ismaili Community, 1866–1966.' University of Central Florida Libraries, 2019.

Tuffaha, L. 'What to the Arab American is election day.' *Protean Magazine*. Available at: https://proteanmag.com/2024/11/05/what-to-the-arab-american-is-election-day/. 2024 (Accessed: 2024).

Walcott, D. *The Antilles: Fragment of Epic Memory.* Farrar, Straus and Giroux, 1993.

Wenzel, J. 'Forest Fictions and Ecological Crises: Reading the Politics of Survival in Mahasweta Devi's "Dhowli"', in *Postcolonial Ecologies: Literatures of the Environment*. Oxford University Press, 2011.

Wong, J. *Going Toward the Ghost: The Poetics of Haunting in Contemporary Asian American Poetry.* University of Washington, 2016.

Woolf, V. *To the Lighthouse*. Union Square, 2023.

Woolf, V. *The Diary of Virginia Woolf*. Volume Three: 1925–1930. Harvest Books, 2020.

Wordsworth, D. *Journals of Dorothy Wordsworth: The Grasmere Journals, 1800–1803*. Oxford University Press, 1971.

Youn, M. *From From*. Carcanet Poetry, 2023.

Zauner, M. *Crying in H Mart*. Knopf, 2022.